WHY DOES EVERYTHING COME IN THREES?

PETER J. KREEFT

Why Does Everything Come in Threes?

(A Short Book about Everything)

IGNATIUS PRESS   SAN FRANCISCO

Unless otherwise indicated, Scripture quotations are from Revised Standard Version of the Bible—Second Catholic Edition (Ignatius Edition) copyright © 2006 National Council of the Churches of Christ in the United States of America. All rights reserved worldwide.

Cover art: Enrique J. Aguilar

Cover design by Enrique J. Aguilar

© 2024 by Ignatius Press, San Francisco
All rights reserved
ISBN 978-1-62164-679-2 (PB)
ISBN 978-1-64229-296-1 (eBook)
Library of Congress Control 2023948187
Printed in the United States of America ∞

CONTENTS

Introduction 7

Chapter One: Why does everything in the universe (the *setting* of our story) come in threes? 19
   Diagrams 1–4 31–32

Chapter Two: Why do the *characters* in our stories, and their powers, come in threes? 33
   Diagrams 5–6 57–58

Chapter Three: Why do the stages of every story's *plot* come in threes? 59

Chapter Four: Why do our greatest *values* and themes of our story come in threes? 71
   Diagram 7 78

Chapter Five: Why does the One God come in three Persons? 87

Chapter Six: The practical "payoff": What difference does it make? 105

Appendix I: A Revolutionary Metaphysics 129
Appendix II: On "IN" 135
Appendix III: A Trinitarian Feminism 145

INTRODUCTION

I'll try to make this introduction short, because most introductions lie. (Perhaps I'm even lying now about my lying.)

Why do most introductions lie? Obviously, to sell the book. It's part of that great enterprise called advertising, the world's oldest profession, which was invented by the Father of Lies to sell his first apple computer to Adam and Eve. He still gets his icon stamped on all his products: the apple with a bite taken out of it. (And if you ask why there's only one bite on his icon when Adam and Eve both took bites out of his apple, it's because the Devil is a male chauvinist sexist pig. Nothing infuriates him more than to get definitively and devastatingly *whupped* by a "mere" woman, the New Eve, as predicted in Genesis 3:15.)

The word that is the main motive power for most advertisements is the word "new". Advertisers, like their Father Below, know how to use this magic word to play on our passions, on our ignorance, and on our boredom with "the same old thing". But this book is *not* a "new" theology of the Trinity. Most "new" theologies are heresies. For the Trinity is not new, except to unbelievers. Nor is it an old and worn-out theology, except to believers who are worn-out. The Trinity is present and eternal, that is, timeless, time-transcending.

(The present is the only dimension of time in which we can touch eternity, because it is the only time dimension in which we can act. Time is like a horizontal line, and eternity is like a vertical line, and the center where the two cross is at the Cross, where eternity impregnated time.)

Not only is this book not a new theology of the Trinity, it is not primarily a theology of the Trinity at all. Insofar as it is about the Trinity itself, in the next to last chapter, it merely summarizes and translates into more ordinary language what the Church has always taught about the Trinity.

It is not an original contribution to systematic theology. To learn about that, go to my betters:

1. to the Scriptures, which are the Word of God to man, not just man's words about God;
2. to the Creeds of the Church, which summarize her Sacred Apostolic Tradition, which she received from Christ and his Apostles and their God-ordained successors, the bishops, who are the jackasses that continue to carry Christ into Jerusalem to carry on his work;
3. to the real theologians, like Augustine and Aquinas;
4. to the saints, Eastern and Western;

5. to the mystics, like the Carmelites; and
6. to effective and faithful apologists like Blaise Pascal, John Henry Newman, Fulton Sheen, Frank Sheed, G.K. Chesterton, and C.S. Lewis. (The clearest and most helpful popular account of the Trinity that I've ever read is Frank Sheed's in *Theology and Sanity*.)

I have deliberately put the only two or three new or revolutionary ideas into the Appendices. Even there, they are corollaries that follow, I believe, from the traditional positions laid out in the rest of the text.

This book is more about the Trinity in the creation than about the Trinity in the Creator; more about the art than about the Artist; and most especially about us, his kids, made in his Trinitarian image.

Because, as Chesterton put it, when he created us, God "broke his own law and made a graven image of himself", we find a Trinitarian structure in each of the dimensions of the story of our lives: (1) the setting, (2) the characters, (3) the plot, and (4) the theme. These are the first four chapters.

And that means not merely Threes but Three-*in-Ones*. The three are one, not merely three; and the one is three, not merely one. Like God, like

Ultimate Reality. Proximate reality reflects ultimate reality, because it has no other place to go to get anything.

☙

We do not call a real person an image of his photograph or portrait, but the reverse. The image reflects the model, the model does not reflect the image. We are made "in the image of God", and the two consequences of that are (1) that we are like God and (2) that God is not like us. Compared to God, we are barely real.

Because of this principle, religious language is full of images, symbols, resemblances, and analogies, but not in the way we usually think. For we are habitually upside down: it is we who are the symbols, and thus it is language about *us*, not God, that is symbolic rather than literal. We are symbols or icons of God, as our bodies are symbols or icons of our souls, rather than vice versa.

For instance, our bodies do not digest literal food. "Soul food" is literal food. Thus when Jesus and his disciples are out in the wilderness without food, and he says, "I have food to eat of which you do not know", and his disciples say, "Has anyone brought him food?" and he answers, "My food is to do the will of him who sent me" (Jn 4:32–34), they do not understand him because they think that

that "soul food" is only a symbol, when in fact it is the food our bodies eat that is the symbol.

And when Jesus says we must eat his flesh and drink his blood, he corrects our natural tendency to interpret that symbolically by saying that "my flesh is food indeed, and my blood is drink indeed" (Jn 6:55). "Give us this day our daily bread" refers first of all to the Eucharist, the true Wonder Bread.

And when we call God our "Father", we are not speaking symbolically but literally. It is human fatherhood that is the symbol. Thus God's Word calls God "the Father, from whom every family in heaven and on earth is named" (Eph 3:14–15), not vice versa. That's what Jesus meant when he said "call no man your father on earth, for you have one Father, who is in heaven" (Mt 23:9).

When we think upside down and backwards, as we habitually do, we forget that we are the symbols, the images, the holy pictures, the icons. Our bodies are cathedrals, temples of the Holy Spirit.

This book explores first of all the symbols: *our* trinities. Then, at the end, God's Trinity.

The basic outline of this first and main part of this book follows the four dimensions of every story: setting, characters, plot, and theme.

Human life is a story. That's why storytelling is the oldest and most universal of all human art forms. No human culture has ever been discovered that did not tell stories. For the human life that surrounds all stories and invents all stories is itself a story.

Christianity is a story. Its essence is composed of real, concrete, literal events in history, things that really happened and were really seen. It is not, like most religions, a set of principles, platitudes, and pontifications. Its theology and morality are reflections on these events, interpretations of these events, commentaries on and corollaries of these events. That's why the books of the Bible, both in the Old Testament and in the New, are classified as historical books first and then "wisdom literature" and prophetic books later. What we confess in the Creeds is mostly facts of history, not first of all abstract eternal truths. "Christ has died, Christ is risen, Christ will come again"—that's it in a nutshell. It is facts, not fictions or fantasies or even laws and principles, that constitute the essence of the Christian faith.

That is true of no other religion. It's true of Judaism, but biblical Judaism is not another religion; it's the religion Christ believed and said he had come to fulfill, not to abolish.

൭

The *setting* of our story is the universe. It is a very large and long setting (about 13.7 billion light-years), and the only characters we know in that story—human beings—and their planet are an unimaginably tiny part of the universe. Yet we are also greater than the universe because we transcend the universe in knowing it and in telling stories about it. This tiny part of the great universe—us—is greater than the whole universe that physically contains it, for we can mentally contain the universe by knowing it and loving it, while it cannot know us or love us. If an atom bomb falls on us and destroys us and billions of others, we are still greater than the bomb, for we know it while it does not know us. We are greater than the whole universe. The part is greater than the whole. A few billion *persons* are greater than quintillions of *things*.

The universe has three dimensions: matter, time, and space. Time has three dimensions: past, present, and future. Space has three dimensions: height, width, and depth.

In chapter 1, we will explore this setting, the Trinity in the universe.

We ourselves are the *characters* in the story, of course, and we all have three dimensions: spirit (which is the source of our relationship to the God above us), soul (which is the source of our relationship to ourselves and others like us), and body (which is the source of our relationship to the universe).

Our souls have three distinctively human powers: mind, will, and heart. They demand and seek three absolute values: truth, goodness, and beauty. Our stories, when they are great enough and long enough, almost always have three main characters who reflect these three powers of the human soul: a prophet or wise man or wizard; a king or ruler or leader; and a priest or self-sacrificing sacramental agent.

In chapter 2, we will explore the Trinity in our own souls and in the stories that reveal ourselves.

❧

The *plot* of our stories, both individual and collective, both secular and sacred, both past and present, is also Trinitarian in structure, temporally. There are three stages to every story: beginning, middle, and end; a set-up, an up-set, and a re-set.

In chapter 3, we will explore the Trinity in the plot of our history and our individual lives as well as the stories we tell.

❧

The most important dimension of our stories is their meaning, their values, their *themes*. The first question children ask about a story is about its theme: "What's that story *about?*"

In chapter 4, we will explore the Trinity in the themes of our stories.

Our stories have horizontal (natural) and vertical (supernatural) dimensions, like a cross. The vertical dimension is religion, our relationship to God, either the true God or false gods. Most of the time this relationship is not conscious to us, subjectively, but it is universal and pervasive, objectively. The "secular", or "worldly" world, which takes up most of our time and space, is suffused throughout with the sacred. The sacred is to the secular what the soul is to the body. The soul is in the whole body, not just in the brain or the pineal gland, as Descartes stupidly thought. (It takes a genius to be really stupid.)

Religion has three aspects: creed, code, and cult, or words, works, and worship. Its God-appointed ministers are prophets, kings, and priests; preachers, rulers, and servers.

In chapter 5, we will explore the Trinitarian structure of our religious relationship to God.

Since all these reflections of the Trinity depend on the Trinity itself, we conclude with a brief and elementary look at the source of all created trinities, namely, the Trinity in the Creator. So in chapter 6, we will explore the source and foundation of all Trinities, the One God.

❧

And in chapter 7, we will explore the practical consequences, corollaries, and applications of this truth, that the structure of God, of Ultimate Reality, is Trinitarian: what difference does that make to our lives? The answer is that it makes the most total and radical difference anything can ever possibly make.

❧

Three philosophical appendices follow, one on the revolution in metaphysics that is implied in the truth that God (or Being Itself, Ultimate Reality) is love, one on the ubiquity and profundity of the little word "in", and one on the metaphysics of women.

❧

So now that I have let the cat out of the bag and told you everything that you are going to meet on your journey of exploration if you read this book, you can decide *not* to hop onto my boat without the fear that you will have missed something new and surprising that you were not warned about.

Or you can decide to come aboard and explore the common Trinitarian structure of everything, of the whole universe and the human life in it of which you are a part, and also explore the basis of its structure in exploring that of its divine architect.

For what else *is* there to explore, anyway? Nothing. And nothing has no structure. What can you say about nothing? Nothing.

Chapter One

Why does everything in the universe (the *setting* of our story) come in threes?

This is by far the most abstract and probably boring chapter in the book. Please feel free to skip it, to skip around in it, or to leave it when you are so bored or confused as to be frustrated.

The setting is the least important of the dimensions of our life's story, as it is in most stories. When we die and leave this whole universe, we will totally change the setting of our story ("Behold, I make all things new", "a new heaven and a new earth" (Rev 21:5, 1)—but not the characters (us) or the essential plot (love story) or the themes (truth, goodness, and beauty).

The basic structure of the universe is mathematical. Arithmetic is one-dimensional, plane geometry is two-dimensional, solid geometry is three-dimensional, and physics is four-dimensional because it deals with motion: with bodies not only in three-dimensional space but also in time.

Within space, lines are one-dimensional, shapes are two-dimensional, and solid bodies are three-dimensional.

❧

Arithmetic is more fundamental than geometry because it does not presuppose material space. We find a trinity in arithmetic. Arithmetically, three is the reconciliation and synthesis of "the one and the many", i.e., of one (which is *not* two) and two (which is *not* one). Three is the "higher synthesis" (to use Hegelian language) that reconciles the "thesis" of one with the "antithesis" of many (for two is the foundation of manyness). It does this in two ways: first, it adds, or synthesizes, the number one, the basis of oneness, and the number two, the basis of manyness; and secondly, the number three is *one* number, one three, but it is also *three* ones. A remote echo of one God, three Persons.

As the reconciliation of oneness and manyness, the number three symbolizes the alternative to both monism (only one) and pluralism (only many) philosophically, and of both monistic pantheism (the denial of God's transcendence) and pluralistic deism (the denial of God's immanence) theologically. It is the mathematical analogy to the theological mystery of God's simultaneous immanence and transcendence. It both refutes the falsehoods and synthesizes or reconciles the half-truths of both pantheism and deism, and of both monism and pluralism.

Three is not merely one of the infinite series of positive integers, one among many. It is unique in reconciling oneness and manyness. Like God.

Turning from arithmetic to geometry, a very simple, obvious, and concrete trinity in the geometry of the universe is the triangle.

No other geometrical figure is the basis for a whole mathematical science (trigonometry).

No other geometrical figure is the most stable architectural building block, both in flat space and in curved space (geodesic domes).

No other geometrical figure encloses a space with fewer lines.

The mathematical trinities are more fundamental than the physical trinities we will explore next, because mathematics, unlike physics, applies also to angels, who, until and unless they don human costumes, are pure spirits and immaterial, lacking matter, space, and the kind of time that is measured by the movement of matter through space. (There is also a spiritual time, as we shall see in a moment.)

※

Physics as well as mathematics is Trinitarian in structure. The most obvious and all-pervasive reason why the physical universe is Trinitarian is that matter, time, and space are its three dimensions.

They are relative to each other, as the Persons of the Trinity are relative to each other: the Father is not first who he is *and then* related to the Son; his whole Person is his relation to the Son. And the correlative is true of the Son in his relation to the Father. And the Holy Spirit is not first the Spirit *and then* the Spirit of the Father and the Son, or of the Father through the Son, but his whole Person is that relationship.

So relationship is the absolute. Paradoxically, relativity is the absolute! As we shall explore later, that is the abstract philosophical version of "God *is* love."

And if you did not understand that great theological mystery, welcome to the human race. It is not a bad thing to state something that you know is profoundly and importantly true even if you do not understand it. Even a tiny glimmer of light about the most important things is more important than total and adequate light on lesser things. Unlike God, we have to choose between those two alternatives of profundity *or* clarity. God doesn't. We understand numbers far better than we understand persons, but when you are on your deathbed, your regrets will have everything to do with your personal relationships and little or nothing to do with your mathematics. We will regret not saying "I love you" more than we will regret not solving equations.

The setting, the characters, and the plot are the three main aspects of every story. The themes are more important, but they are the timeless dimension; the other three dimensions are temporal. The universe is the setting of our story, we are the characters, and the events of the story are the plot. So our lives, as stories, are three-dimensional.

Within the setting of the story there are also three main dimensions or aspects: matter, space, and time. Events (the plot) are movements of matter through space and time.

And within time itself, we again find three dimensions: past, present, and future.

Space also has three dimensions: height, width, and depth.

Matter also has three dimensions: energy, mass, and motion.

So it's trinities within trinities "all the way down" and "all the way up" into God.

❧

Height, width, and depth are the three dimensions of the one single dimension of space. It is space itself that contains these three spatial dimensions. They are not *parts* of space but *dimensions* of it. Space is not composed of or *made out of* three dimensions. It is *three-dimensional*. It is not as if $1+1+1=3$ but as if $3=1+1+1$. When we say space has three dimensions, we are not expressing a real synthesis but a mental analysis. We are not adding height, width, and depth to make space but dividing space into its three dimensions, mentally.

This is like the three Persons of the Trinity, who are not triplets. They are the One God. Triplets are parts of a family. God has no parts. Space also has no parts. Of course the three Persons of the Trinity are not *dimensions* of God, and the three dimensions of space are not persons. Not all trinities are the same; "trinity" is analogical.

Unlike space, matter has parts that are actually separate and that can be divided actually and objectively, like a slice of bread cut with a knife, and not divided merely in thought, subjectively, as dimensions can be. Matter has "extensions", or parts outside of other parts. Space itself does not have parts, though we can impose parts upon it conceptually by mentally dividing it into parts. But parts are not the same as dimensions. Space has an indefinite number of parts but only three dimensions.

With regard to time, some languages (e.g., Greek) distinguish between physical time (*kronos*) and spiritual or mental time (*kairos*); others (e.g., English) do not. Physical time is measured by the external universe, by the movement of matter through space (e.g., days and years are measured by the earth's rotation and revolution around the sun). Spiritual time is measured by purpose and desire, by the internal universe.

A quick look at the three dimensions of physical time: past, present, and future:

All physical time was once future (at the beginning of time).

And all physical time will some day be past (at the end of time).

And all events in physical time are present rather than past or future at some time, for time is, lives, or exists, only in the present. Past time is dead (no longer present), and future time is unborn (not yet present).

Yet time, like God, is also one, and not only three. It is the one time, it is time itself, that is past and present and future. Time is one thing, one reality, one dimension, not three that are then added or synthesized. *We* analyze time, which is one, into its three dimensions of past, present, and future. In that way, time is partially subjective, as Augustine discovered. It takes a mind, a subject, a person, to hold past and present and future together in the lived present of consciousness. They are held together only in a mind, not in objective reality in the physical universe, where they are not mutually exclusive.

But time is not *merely* subjective; it is a dimension of objective reality. Even before we discovered them, dinosaurs were real and came before humans. And the *division* between the three dimensions of time is also partly objective: the past really is past, not present or future, and the present really is present, not past or future, and the future really is future, not past or present.

Again, this is like the three Persons of the Trinity. The Father is not the Son or the Spirit, and the Son is not the Father or the Spirit, and the Spirit is not the Father or the Son, yet God is the one God, not three Gods, and the one God *is* three Persons. (See Diagram 1, p. 31 below.)

❧

Matter itself is also Trinitarian, for it is energy and mass and motion, the standard of which is the speed of light. Paradoxically, the universal *constant* is the speed of light's *movement*.

The unity of the three dimensions of matter are expressed in the formula $E=mc^2$; energy equals mass times the speed of light multiplied by itself. In this formula for matter, we find both its unity (the "equals") and its trinity (energy, mass, and motion, at the speed of light).

Energy is in a way the most fundamental, since matter is congealed or potential energy, or energy is uncongealed or released matter. Energy may be the physical expression of the act of existence itself, which is the heart of Being, and is indefinable because there is nothing more fundamental than "is". (This priority of the act of existence is explained best by the metaphysics of Saint Thomas Aquinas.) In some ways, matter is to energy what essence is to existence.

Physical energy and spiritual energy are not the same, nor are they simply and absolutely different, but one of them (physical energy) is analogous to, or an image of, the other, as the body is to the soul.

The three dimensions of matter are distinct and irreducible to each other, so that the threeness cannot be eliminated or reduced to the oneness; yet they are also relative to each other in the oneness of matter, so that the oneness cannot be eliminated or reduced to the threeness.

So just as with time and space, matter is not merely threefold but also one. Like the Trinity:

The Father is God.

The Son is God.

The Spirit is God.

The Father is not the Son. He is the Father *of* the Son. He eternally "begets" the Son.

The Son is not the Father. He is the Son *of* the Father. He is eternally "begotten" of the Father. He, not the Father or the Spirit, becomes incarnate, dies, and rises.

The Spirit is not the Father or the Son. He eternally (timelessly) "proceeds" *from* the Father and the Son, or from the Father through the Son. He is "sent" by the Father and the Son into time, and into us.

In terms of our experience of God, the Father is God "outside" us and "above" us; the Son is God "beside" us as one of us—we are his "brothers" and his "Body"—and the Spirit is God "inside" us. These are three stages of intimacy, which is the aim of love. In that sense, the analogy is a good one. But the geometrical analogy of outside, beside, and inside is imperfect because it judges God—the God who is not relative to us and who is not defined by space—in terms relative to us and our experience and our "space"—and also because all three Persons are in all three "places".

The revelations of God first as the Father and then as the Son and then as the Holy Spirit are the three stages of salvation history, revealed first in Israel and documented in the Old Testament, and then in the Incarnation and documented in the Gospels, and then in the Church, and documented in the rest of the New Testament.

And the three dimensions of the universe also have this same structure in relation to each other; and each within itself again manifests the same or similar structure as the Trinitarian God. (Compare Diagrams 2 through 4 with Diagram 1, see pp. 31–32, below.)

And if you think that is a coincidence, I have a time-share in Florida that I would like to sell you.

An even more fundamental philosophical trinity is the ontological or metaphysical trinity of being, non-being, and becoming, as in Hegel's dialectic. I hope you will excuse or indulge me for a very short trip into the philosophy of a notoriously difficult but profound thinker, who was *not* a Christian, even though his whole philosophy has a Trinitarian structure.

The structure is the waltz-like "dialectic" of thesis, antithesis, and synthesis. To take the most fundamental example, in metaphysics: If we begin with nothing, with non-being, as our "thesis", we see that it makes sense only relative to being, as the negation or opposite of being, as our "antithesis". And if instead we begin with being as our thesis, we see that being makes sense only if it is the negation or opposite of non-being as our antithesis. And then we notice that that opposition and negation and movement of mind from non-being to being and from being to non-being is itself a third concept, namely, becoming or movement or relationship, which is a synthesis of being and non-being. So even at the level of the most abstract concepts possible, we observe a kind of Trinitarian structure.

However, this philosophical Hegelian trinity is of a different structure from the theological Trinity. The theological Trinity is not a "synthesis" of "thesis" and "antithesis". Hegel's trinity applies only to time, both mental (the *concepts* of being and non-being and becoming) and physical (his philosophy of history and human life).

At this point many of you will thank me for making this chapter the shortest. And since your interest interests me, I will now do to this chapter what God will do to this universe at the end of time, when he will end this one and make another universe ("new heavens and a new earth"), with another kind of matter and body, with another kind of time, and with another kind of space. And I hope to see you there, where we will have a good laugh at this book.

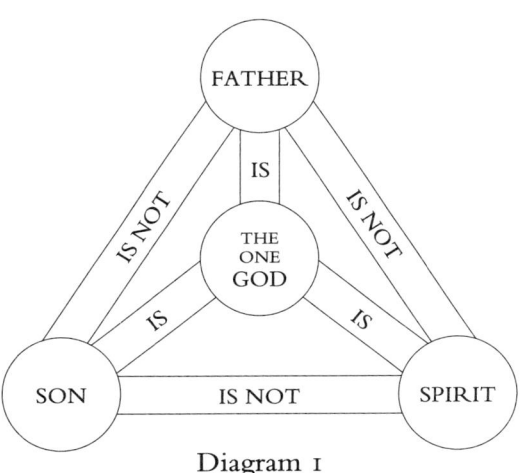

Diagram 1

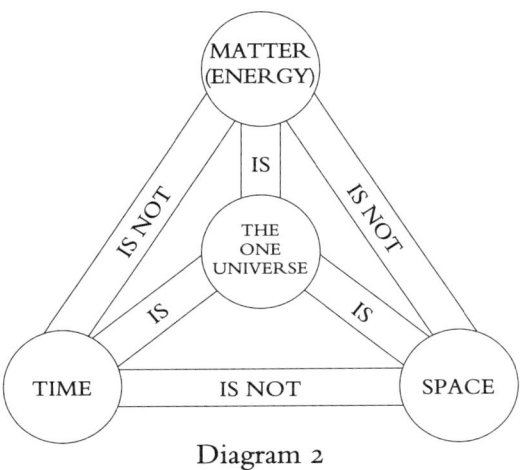

Diagram 2

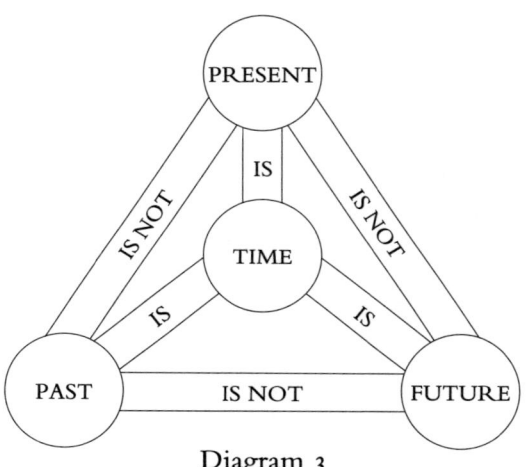

Diagram 3

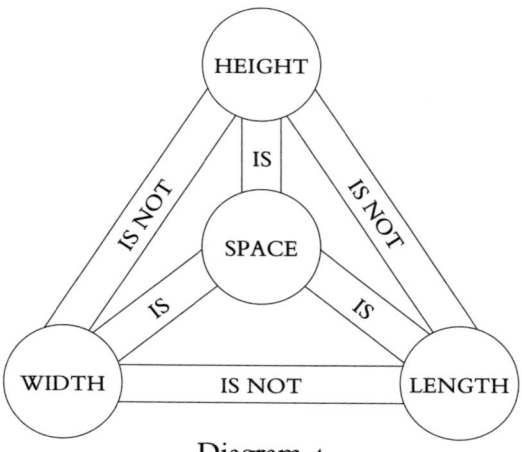

Diagram 4

Chapter Two

Why do the *characters* in our stories, and their powers, come in threes?

I must warn you not to look for a one-to-one Trinitarian parallel in this chapter, as if one of the three characters in our stories somehow symbolizes, reflects, or represents the Father, another the Son, and another the Spirit. The three characters are going to exemplify the divinely instituted authorities of prophets, kings, and priests, as well as our three spiritual powers of mind, will, and heart; but the Father is not more prophetic or more intellectual, nor is the Son more kingly or volitional, nor is the Spirit more priestly or affective, than the other two Persons in the Trinity. None of the Persons lacks anything good; each has the whole divine nature. There is indeed a Trinitarian reflection, but it is not simple, direct, and one to one.

Functionally, it is the Spirit who inspires the prophets, the Son is our High Priest, and the Father is the King of the universe. But the Father has given all authority to the Son (Mt 28:18), and the Son has entrusted his ministry to the Spirit (Jn 16:13), and both work to glorify the Father (Jn 5:30), so that even though there is some kind of a "specialization" in the work of the Three, that specialized work is also inclusive and not exclusive; passed on and not kept. For that is what Love does. It "passes on", rather than "keeping", itself.

Families

The essence of drama is the relationship between persons. The most important, most dramatic, most joyful, and most painful of all relationships between persons are family relationships. The family is the most essential structure of human relationships. Thus the decay or decline of the family is the single most serious of all tragedies and the Devil's single most effective way to corrupt human society, culture, and civilization.

There are three irreducible and natural roles in any family: father, mother, and child. Every child exists because his father and his mother became a "we" biologically.

The Holy Family was a true family even though Joseph was not Jesus' biological father, since Jesus' Father was his heavenly Father, thus giving him a divine nature, and his mother was his earthly mother, thus giving him a human nature.

God himself is a kind of family. He is not like a family, but a family is like him. God the Father and God the Son are in a relationship that is imaged physically in the created order by the male-female relationship. It is this *relationship*, rather than a single individual—in other words, "Adam" as mankind rather than "Adam" as the individual who stands over against Eve—that Scripture identifies as "the image of God", according to Genesis 1:27 ("the image of God ... male and female"). This is explored profoundly in Pope Saint John Paul II's *Theology of the Body*.

And like God himself, this relationship is essentially creative: from it, from the oneness-in-twoness and twoness-in-oneness of the parents, emerges the child. In the Trinity, it is not material and biological, of course. God is not either male or female because God is not a biological being. And God is not in time. But in God, too, this relationship is "creative", for the Holy Spirit proceeds (timelessly) from the Father and the Son together, so that the human, physical, and temporal love between husband and wife from which "proceeds" a child is the sacred image of the fact that the Spirit timelessly "proceeds from" the love between Father and Son. Just as the Father's self-knowledge is so real and complete that it is a divine Person, eternally "begotten", so their love is so real and complete that it, too, is a divine Person, the Spirit, who eternally "proceeds" from their union, as the totality of their love. That is why the human family is in one way a closer relation to the Trinity than any of the other created trinities: because it is the unity of three concrete *persons* (characters) rather than three abstract "dimensions" or "stages" or "kinds" or "elements" or "aspects".

Three main characters

Not all stories, but most of our great and long stories, have three main characters.

Inside families, the three main characters are, of course, father, mother, and child. But also outside families, protagonists come typically in threes. As we shall see, they correspond to prophets, kings, and priests, the offices and authorities instituted by the Trinitarian God, because they correspond to the three distinctively human powers of the rational soul, namely, the mind, the will, and the heart (the spiritual emotions).

The title of this chapter contains an empirical assumption, which ought to be proved before we go any farther: the assumption that this pattern of three main characters, one of whom is like a prophet, one like a king, and one like a priest, is typical in our stories if they are both great and long.

It is not that *all* stories have three main characters, for two reasons. First, most stories are too short to do justice to more than one protagonist.

And second, some long stories, like *The Epic of Gilgamesh*, *The Aeneid*, *The Odyssey*, and *The Divine Comedy*, center on a single character (Gilgamesh, Aeneas, Ulysses, and Dante himself). The single protagonist often manifests all three of these functions in himself. But almost all long and great stories do have one protagonist who specializes in wisdom, one in rule and authority, and one in humble service—in other words, a prophetic, a kingly, and a priestly protagonist.

The greatest book of all is of course the Bible, and in it God established these three institutional and social externalizations of our three individual spiritual powers in his chosen people Israel; and when he became incarnate, in Christ, he fulfilled all three: Christ is the supreme prophet, the supreme king, and the supreme priest.

In the Gospels, Jesus calls many disciples, but within them only the Twelve Apostles, and within them again only three in his "inner circle" who accompany him both to his life's greatest height of glory (the Transfiguration) and its greatest depth of agony (Gethsemane). They are Saint John, who writes the most profound, most philosophical, and most mystical of the Gospels; Saint Peter, whom Christ appoints as the "rock" on which he will build his Church and who always appears as the leader and spokesman for all the Apostles; and Saint James, who (especially if he is the same James who wrote the epistle) is a practical, hobbit-like everyday moralist.

In Dostoyevsky's *The Brothers Karamazov*, the greatest novel ever written (I say that dogmatically and authoritatively!), the three protagonists and brothers are Ivan, the philosopher and "intellectual", Dmitri, the soldier with a strong ego, and Alyosha, the saint who ministers in a priestly way to all the other characters.

We begin to see already (and this will be confirmed by subsequent examples) that the third is the hardest to define. And there is a necessary reason for this, since this third public office or function manifests and exemplifies the third power of the soul, the "heart", the affections, passions, or emotions, which are the most subjective, the most diverse, and the most hard to define of our spiritual powers.

In the original *Star Trek*, the most philosophical of all TV serials, and one of the most popular, the three most important characters, who are constantly interacting, are Mr. Spock, the brilliant and logical science officer, Kirk, the courageous and egotistic captain of the spaceship, and "Bones" McCoy, the compassionate, humble doctor. The starship is called the *Enterprise*, and it is an allegory for the human soul, and its missions are an allegory for human life.

In *The Lord of the Rings*, which three popular polls picked as the greatest book of the twentieth century (and one poll as the greatest book of the second *millennium!*), the three main protagonists are three "Christ-figures" who give themselves away in different ways, and even go through death, in different ways, to save Middle-Earth: Gandalf (the Wizard, the prophet, the wise man), Aragorn (the literal King), and Frodo the Hobbit, who performs the priestly function of a concrete sacramental sacrifice of himself by his trip to the Crack of Doom in Mordor, like Christ's trip to Hell on the Cross.

In *Jaws*, the highest grossing movie of all time at the time, we have the trio of Hooper, the scientist, Quint, the captain of the *Orca*, and Brodie, the humble, ordinary landlubber. No one else counts much in the plot.

In *Harry Potter*, we have another trio: Hermione is the brightest and bookiest, Harry is the leader, and Ron is the ordinary semi-Muggle.

In *The Wizard of Oz*, the three protagonists are the scarecrow, who needs a brain, the cowardly lion, who needs a courageous will, and the tin man, who needs a heart.

So from the highest classical epics to the lowest popular movies, we see the same pattern repeated. This is obviously not a coincidence. Even if you are not a Christian and do not want to trace it back to the Trinity in God, you have at least to trace it back to the trinity in the human self or psyche or soul or spirit. Nearly every map of the human soul has some version of these three powers, even the most extremely opposite ones like Plato's (reason, will or "spirited part", and passions) versus Freud's (super-ego, ego, and id). And even if you believe that we created God in our own image rather than vice versa, you cannot not-see the universal Trinitarian pattern. (See Diagram 5, p. 57 below.)

This Trinitarian pattern is typically Christian. For we see it in almost all Christian epics and in no pagan epics. Pagan epics always have a single protagonist (Gilgamesh, Aeneas, Achilles, Ulysses, Beowulf), or at most two, if the protagonist has a single friend or lover (Enkidu, Dido). He is never one of three, like Christ in the divine nature and like the protagonists in Christian-influenced epics such as the many examples mentioned above.

There is often a prophet or wizard figure in pagan epics (e.g., Tiresias in *Oedipus*), but he is peripheral, not a central character, not a protagonist himself. Neither is the priest figure, who sometimes is identical with the prophet and sometimes in contrast and opposition to him, like the "Priest" vs. the "Fox" in C. S. Lewis' *Till We Have Faces*, which is a Christian-inspired epic laid in a pre-Christian culture.

Also, the pagan protagonist is almost always a literal warrior. His heroism consists of force and violence, or at least practical cleverness (e.g., Ulysses). For when we create our idols, our false gods, we create them in our own image; but when the true God appears, we are turned upside down and our violence is confronted with nonviolence, mercy, love, and sacrifice, and with God's appeal to our free choice rather than fear and force.

This historical fact is obviously not a coincidence but philosophically and theologically significant. It was not usually deliberately planned, strategized, and worked out by the Christian authors, but it was subconscious and intuitive; the Trinity was there in their Christian "collective unconscious" before it was there in the characters they saw in front of their vision with the eyes of their creative imagination. It was in the characters because it was first of all in their authors, and it was in their eyes (their creative imagination) because it was first of all in their I's (their soul's image-of-God trinity).

The three powers of the soul

Our stories are stories about ourselves, about human beings; and obviously the structure of the characters in our stories reflects the structure in ourselves. The three distinctively human powers that make us unique in the universe, that make us persons instead of things, subjects instead of objects, spiritual as well as biological, conscious of self instead of only of the world outside us and, therefore, responsible moral agents, are mind, will, and heart.

By the "heart" I mean not merely and simply the emotions as such, for the higher animals also share some of the same emotions we do, e.g., contentment and discontent, anger, affection, and even spontaneous and instinctive charity, though not the charity that is a free choice. I use the word "heart" as Scripture does, i.e., as the source of the spiritual and not merely animal feelings, feelings that are "intentional", i.e., *about* something other than themselves, and therefore have a moral dimension, are good or bad, correct or incorrect, true or false, rightly ordered or disordered—e.g., wonder, awe, boredom, gratitude, envy, moral outrage, love and appreciation of beauty, creative imagination, duty and responsibility, guilt or guiltlessness, deliberate hatred or affection, pity or cruelty, envy or praise, rejoicing or sorrowing. The sentiments or affections are very many, very diverse, and very powerful motivators.

It was Plato who first made a map of the soul, and it was Trinitarian. The one soul had three powers, three functions, three "faculties".

First, there was the mind, intellect, or reason. This meant, for Plato and for almost all premodern thinkers, something broader than logical reasoning or calculating, and something much broader than the whole modern scientific method. It included what Aristotle later called the three acts of the mind: intellectual intuition, "simple apprehension", or *understanding* the meaning of a concept (e.g., "man"); *judging* a proposition to be true or false (e.g., "All men are mortal"); and *reasoning* or arguing from some propositions (premises) to others (a conclusion), whether inductive or deductive (e.g., "All men are mortal, and I am a man, therefore I am mortal"). (See Diagram 6, p. 58 below.)

Second, there was what Plato called "the spirited part", which was a primitive conception of the will. For Plato, it was almost identical with the irascible appetites. Aristotle had a much clearer concept of the will and its freedom or voluntariness.

Third, there were the passions or emotions, of which Plato also had a fairly primitive conception; he called them simply the "appetites".

But these are all powers of the rational, i.e., human, soul or psyche, not of the body alone, and they distinguish us from the "brutes" (the clear but insulting word for nonrational animals). The word "soul" was also used in a broader way by premodern thinkers than it usually is by us today: it meant "principle (source) of life". Only humans have *rational* souls, i.e., souls that could perform the three acts of the mind (above) and free acts of the will. Animals have only "sensitive souls" and, like even plants, "vegetative souls".

One may perhaps semi-seriously ask whether the current generation of iPhone addicts or technological contemplatives who "veg out" as "couch potatoes" are higher or lower than the animals on this natural hierarchy. Are potatoes with ingrown eyes higher than dogs who wag their tails in affection at others? When you come home, how are you greeted by your dog? How are you greeted by your addicted teenager?

Okay, I know I shouldn't have put that snarky paragraph in, but it gave you a tiny little "ha" smile, didn't it?

Plato deduced that the soul must have these three powers or forces from the experience of inner conflict. We often know, with one power (the intellect), what is true or good, but we are also drawn by something else (the passions, appetites, or desires) toward something else that is contrary to truth or to our true good. And sometimes we follow the first of those forces or influences, and sometimes we follow the second, so there must be some third power that casts the deciding vote, so to speak, that accounts for which one we follow. For we do not always follow the strongest of the first two forces. And that third force is what Plato called "the spirited part" and Aristotle, later, and more clearly, the will, which is what makes an act voluntary (that is, willed, and thus in our power and responsibility) rather than involuntary.

Three virtues

Each of these special powers needs a special virtue. The virtue of the reason (intellect, mind) is prudence, or practical wisdom, the wisdom to know the truth, especially the truth about the true good.

The virtue of the "spirited part" (will) is the courage to fight, within and without, for what we know is right and against what we know is wrong.

And the virtue of the "appetites" (emotions) is moderation or self-control, being rightly ordered by the truth known by the intellect or mind or reason. "Rightly ordered" means neither "suppressed" nor obeyed uncritically as one obeys a tyrant.

And when each power does its proper job with its proper virtue, we have Plato's definition of personal justice. Justice is more than just rewards and punishments; it is rightness or righteousness or the right ordering of the whole soul. Justice is to the soul what health is to the body.

These are the "four cardinal virtues" that are necessary as the hinge ("carde") on which all other virtues turn because they perfect and harmonize the three distinctively human spiritual powers. They are cross-cultural and have multi-millenial staying power because they are inherent in human nature, not ideological artifices.

Three classes in society

That is why in Plato's *Republic*, the just state, the well-ordered state, the state that reflects and perfects human nature, has three natural "classes" of people who specialize in each of these three functions and powers. The philosopher-kings (and philosopher-queens) are the thinkers, the wise law-*makers*; the guardians or auxiliaries are the courageous warriors, the law-*enforcers* (soldiers and perhaps also intellectual soldiers, including media, artists, and journalists); and the masses, the producers and consumers of property, are the law-*abiders*. In their special social functioning, the rulers especially need wisdom, the soldiers courage, and the producers self-control, but of course all individuals need not just one but all four cardinal virtues to have individually healthy souls.

These are the three essential public functions in every society, even those that are not divided into three actual classes of people. For Plato, it was human nature that arranged people into these three classes. They were not hereditary or voted on politically. Nor were they based on race or gender or wealth.

The social and political details of Plato's supposedly ideal state in the *Republic* are controversial and highly questionable, and history has shown many problems with imitations of it. But history has also shown the staying power of his psychology. We have progressed to much more adequate notions of the will and the passions than Plato's, but nearly every other map of the psyche after Plato's has had this same Trinitarian structure, even when it has been far more sophisticated and even when the relationship among the three powers has been very different from what it was in Plato.

For instance, in Freud all reasoning is merely rationalizing of the passions, which for him are the true self. For Freud, all our notions of the good and our conscience's impetus to obey them are merely unconscious reflections of what society (other people) wants us to do. Yet despite these and other serious differences with Plato (e.g., Freud is a materialist and an atheist), Freud's "super-ego", "id", and "ego" correspond fairly closely to Plato's mind, passions, and will ("spirited part"), even though their authority and their relationships to each other differ.

And the "cardinal virtues" that regulate these three powers of the soul and their integration have remained cardinal, or foundational, for 2400 years, though significantly added to by Aristotle, by Christianity, by medieval philosophers, and by modern psychology.

As we shall explore more deeply in the chapter on themes, or values, these three powers of the soul are powers of apprehending, attaining, or relating to the three goals or goods or values or ideals that all of us want, and want without limit: truth, goodness, and beauty, the natural or "proper" objects of mind, will, and heart.

Three dimensions of each power

Within each of these three powers, we further find three aspects or dimensions. (Trinities within trinities again!) One dimension is subjective, one is objective, and one is relational. There is the subjective, personal power to attain the object; and there is the object itself; and there is the act that relates the subject and the object, the subject touching or attaining or uniting with the object. This sounds very abstract, but its examples are concrete and clear:

With regard to the mind, we have the subject's power to know the truth, the objective truth to be known, and the act of knowing it.

With regard to the will, we have the willer, the willed, and the willing: the choice of the good (whether the true good or only the apparent good), the good willed, and the willing of it.

With regard to the heart, we have the lover, the loved, and the loving. We also have the heart's power to invent or appreciate and enjoy something beautiful, the objective beauty to be invented or appreciated and enjoyed, and the act of inventing or appreciating and enjoying it.

The body's sensory powers reflect this structure, too: there is the sensory power to know some shape or color or sound or smell or taste, that is, the power to perceive with the senses some physical aspect of some physical object; and there is the thing itself to be perceived; and there is the experience of actually perceiving it.

The body's physical desires as well as its perceptions also reflect this Trinitarian structure: there are the physical appetites, or desiring powers; the instinctively desired objects of desire, like food and sleep and sex; and the act of desiring or enjoying the object by the subject.

Surprisingly, there seems to be no equivalent in the body to the appreciation and creation of beauty.

Animals are something a *little* bit like scientists or philosophers, though they are not really scientists or philosophers; and they are a *little* bit like saints and moralists, though they are not really saints or moralists; but they are not apparently even a little bit like creative artists or appreciators of beauty. Even the most intelligent ape cannot appreciate the difference between a vacuum cleaner and a symphony orchestra.

Neither can some of our so-called musicians, like John Cage, apparently. But his vacuum cleaner music was in fact a deliberate human joke, or a deliberate attack on beauty. He could not really abandon his humanity even if he wanted to, just as a suicide cannot kill his soul even if he tries to. To imitate a machine is something a machine cannot do. Nor can an animal deliberately imitate an animal. An ape cannot ape an ape. We can imitate animals, but they can't imitate us. We can laugh at them, but they can't laugh at us. Imitating and laughing-at are distinctively human acts because they are both forms of self-transcendence, of standing outside your own skin and even outside of your soul. They are mild out-of-body and out-of-mind experiences.

Three dimensions of language

We find Plato's Trinitarian psychology even behind our language, with its distinction between declarative sentences (truth-claims, addressed to the mind), imperative sentences (commands, addressed to the will), and exclamatory sentences (expressions of emotion).

There are also three different kinds of parts of speech: nouns, and the adjectives that modify them; verbs, and the adverbs that modify them; and conjunctions and prepositions, which relate nouns or verbs to other nouns or verbs. Ontologically, this reflects three categories of being, three kinds of realities: substances, acts, and relations.

Three acts of the mind

And we find the Trinitarian structure again *within* the mind—trinities within trinities—in the "three acts of the mind" that are the basis for Aristotle's commonsense logic. The mind can (1) apprehend, intuit, comprehend, or understand; it can (2) judge; and it can (3) reason, argue, calculate, or prove. This has been mentioned before, and it is very simple, basic, and obvious; but because it is so rarely taught anymore today, it is profitable to go over it again. It is summarized in Diagram 6, p. 58.

1. The aspect or dimension of reality that is the object of the mental act of understanding (or, technically, "simple apprehension") is an *essence*, a form, the *nature* of some thing or event or situation, the answer to the question "*what* is it?" This is expressed

in a *term*, like "man" or "apple" or "red". A term can be the subject or predicate of a proposition, which is the expression of a judgment.

2. The aspect or dimension of reality that is the object of the mental act of judging is the *existence* (or non-existence, in the case of a negative judgment) of some thing or event or situation. This is expressed by the copula "is" or "is not". E.g., "apples are red" or "man is not an apple."

3. The aspect or dimension of reality that is the object of the mental act of reasoning is a *cause* or reason or explanation for a thing or event. E.g., "it must have rained *because* the streets are wet" or "the streets are wet *because* it rained." We can reason from cause to effect or from effect to cause.

1. The mental product of the act of understanding is a *concept*, e.g., "man" or "mortal".

2. The mental product of the act of judging is a *judgment*, a truth-claim, e.g., "All men are mortal."

3. The mental product of the act of reasoning is an *argument*, e.g., "All men are mortal, and Socrates is a man, therefore Socrates is mortal."

1. Concepts are expressed logically in *terms* (e.g., "man" or "mortal"). Terms are neither true nor false and neither logically valid nor invalid. They are clear or unclear.

2. Judgments are expressed logically in *propositions* (e.g., "all men are mortal"). Propositions are either true or false, but not logically valid or invalid. It is their *terms* that are clear or unclear and the *arguments* that the judgments are parts of that are logically valid or invalid.

3. Arguments are expressed in various logical structures, the commonest, simplest, and clearest of them being *syllogisms* (e.g., "All men are mortal, and Socrates is a man, therefore Socrates is mortal.") Arguments are either logically valid or invalid if they are deductive arguments. If they are inductive arguments, they are more or less probable, i.e., their conclusions are shown to be more or less probably true.

1. Terms are expressed in various languages in words or phrases that are less than sentences; they can be the subjects or predicates of sentences.

2. Propositions are expressed in declarative sentences.

3. Arguments are expressed in logically connected sentences in paragraphs.

1. The goal of understanding is clarity and distinctness (non-ambiguity).

2. The goal of judging is truth and the avoidance of falsehoods.

3. The goal of reasoning is valid proofs, demonstrations that if the premises are true, the truth of the conclusion must necessarily follow.

CHARACTERS

1. The opposite of clarity is ambiguity.
2. The opposite of truth is falsehood.
3. The opposite of logical proof is logical fallacy, fake proof. The rules of logic consist largely in rules for detecting different forms of fallacy.

These are the three logical checkpoints of any argument. Think of the three checkpoints of a spy's mission to carry documents, during the Cold War, from East Berlin to West Berlin through the Berlin Wall. There are three checkpoints: the Communist one east of the Wall, the United Nations one at the Wall, and the Western one west of the Wall. If the spy fails to pass any one of the three checkpoints, his mission fails. The mission symbolized here is to prove some truth. If there are any ambiguous terms, false premises, or logical fallacies in the "proof", the argument fails in its mission to prove the conclusion to be true. If there are no ambiguous terms, false premises, or logical fallacies, the argument succeeds in that mission.

Therefore the three logical questions to ask about anything are: what it is, whether it is, and why it is.

The answers to these questions reveal three metaphysical (ontological) aspects or dimensions of reality: essence, existence, and cause.

Three aspects of human nature

The usual dividing up of man is into body and soul (this is called dichotomy); but Scripture also, in a few places, such as 1 Thessalonians 5:23 and Hebrews 4:12, divides us up into three: body, soul, and spirit (this is called trichotomy): the body is our being in space, time, and matter; the soul is our being in relation to ourselves, our self-consciousness, and our relations to other self-conscious beings (persons); and the spirit is our being in relation to God, explicitly or implicitly.

Their goals are, respectively, health, happiness, and holiness.

These also correspond fairly well (though not exactly) to Kierkegaard's three "stages on life's way", which he called the "aesthetic", the "ethical", and the "religious" modes of human existence (life). They are also the three stages of self-discovery: of body, of soul, and then of spirit.

The body is our relation to the world, the soul is our relation to ourselves and our conscience, and the spirit is our relation to God. Thus what Kierkegaard calls the "aesthetic" stage is the stage of seeing oneself as the center of reality and seeing all things and even other people as external sources of pleasure, which is usually physical, or at least dependent on the physical world. The good desired here is being pleased, or pleasure (including intellectual pleasures), and the evil to be avoided is the pain of boredom.

The "ethical" stage is the stage of seeing oneself as a responsible person among other persons, and the good here is moral virtue (as in Aristotle) or duty and obedience to moral law (as in Kant) while the evil is vice (as in Aristotle) or moral disobedience (as in Kant).

The "religious" stage is the stage of seeing oneself in relation to God, whether God is anonymous, as in Socrates, or revealed, as in Christianity. Its positive value is faith, and its negative value is sin. Thus "whatever does not proceed from faith is sin" (Rom 14:23).

What does that mean? Why is the opposite of faith not unbelief but sin? Because sin and faith are the two fundamentally opposite relations to God. We are here in the realm of the religious, or the spirit, not just the ethical, or the soul. Belief (and unbelief) is in the mind; it is only the intellectual dimension of faith. It is not sufficient. ("You believe that God is one; you do well. Even the demons believe—and shudder."—Jas 2:19) And the opposite of sin is not virtue but faith, because the opposite of virtue is simply vice. We are there still in the realm of the ethical, not the religious; of soul, not spirit; of immorality, not sin.

Both dichotomy and trichotomy can be useful maps, and I think they can be reconciled if spirit is seen as something like the heart of the soul. Both trichotomy and dichotomy are Trinitarian: trichotomy sees the soul itself as one of our three dimensions, and dichotomy divides the soul itself into its three powers, exemplified by the three typical characters in our epic stories.

All these threes are no accident but inherent in the very nature of human consciousness and human experience. These human trinities are not the very nature of God, but they *reflect or image* the nature of God. They do that dimly, and at a great distance, and with great differences, but they do so pretty obviously. And if you are thinking "coincidence" again, I will try again to sell you that time-share.

	PROPHETIC	KINGLY	PRIESTLY
Gospels	Saint John	Saint Peter	Saint James
Star Trek	Mister Spock	Captain Kirk	Doctor McCoy
The Brothers Karamazov	Ivan	Dmitri	Alyosha
The Lord of the Rings	Gandalf	Aragorn	Frodo
Jaws	Hooper	Quint	Brodie
Harry Potter	Hermione	Harry	Ron
The Wizard of Oz	Scarecrow	Cowardly Lion	Tin Man
Power of the Soul	Mind	Will	Heart
Function in Society	Lawmakers	Law Enforcers	Law Obeyers
Virtue	Wisdom	Courage	Moderation (self-control)
Life-style	Contemplative	Active	Productive
Personality type	Melancholic	Choleric	Sanguine
Yoga	Jnana yoga	Karma yoga	Bhakti yoga
Naval function	Navigator	Captain	Sailors
Absolute value	Truth	Goodness	Beauty, joy

Diagram 5

	1	2	3
Act of the mind	understanding	judging	reasoning
Mental product	concept	judgment	argument
Logical expression	term	proposition	syllogism
Expression in language	word or phrase	declarative sentence	paragraph
Example	man	all men are mortal	all men are mortal Socrates is a man ∴ Socrates is mortal
Good quality	clear	true	logically valid
Bad quality	unclear	false	logically invalid
How to tell	definition	many ways	the laws of logic
Question	what it is	whether it is	why it is
Aspect of reality	essence, form	existence	cause

Diagram 6

Chapter Three

Why do the stages of every story's *plot* come in threes?

Our first two chapters were about static, timeless, structural trinities. Plots unfold only in time. But time also reflects eternity (Plato defined time as "the moving image of eternity"), though not in the same way as one static structure reflects another. This chapter is about dynamic, temporal trinities that function in time as plots.

The ultimate reason why there are three stages in every story's plot is that they are the stages of our relationship with God ("salvation history") and the three stages of God's divine revelation. All three are found in Genesis 3. (1) It begins in the wholly-and-simply-good world God created, the "Garden of Eden." (2) It then moves to the Fall, the origin of human evil. (3) And then begins, immediately, the long story of God redeeming ("buying back") mankind, the first announcement of which is the "pro-to-gospel", the first "good news" in

Genesis 3:15, of the Christ, the Messiah, the Promised and Anointed One, the Second Adam, who would come through the free-willed "yes" of Mary, the Second Eve, and would crush the head of the Satanic serpent. And he would do it through his very Achilles heel that the serpent would wound, on the Cross: his mortal human nature, his mortal human Body and its Blood ("for the life of the flesh is in the blood"—Lev 17:11). Sacrifice is the one weapon the Devil cannot mimic.

But we find trinities not only in this religious plot but in all plots.

Sometimes the three stages of a long story play out in trilogies: three novels, plays, or movies. Three is much more common than two or four or any other number. Take movies: two of the most successful movies of all time are trilogies: *The Lord of the Rings* and *The Godfather*.

There have been a number of attempts to enumerate all the kinds of plots that stories have. They have been classified into twelve, into seven, and into three. I "classify" them into one. All stories have a single plot, and it is Trinitarian. All stories have three stages, not two or four: a beginning, a middle, and an end. These are necessary and irreducible.

When stories are told in a strictly sequential and chronological order, these three stages are told sequentially. Even when there are flashbacks and backstories, and/or anticipations or views of the future, the events themselves are always sequential, because time is a one-way street.

The content of the stages is as universal as their number. Always, first a situation is set up, then it is upset, and then it is reset, either successfully (in "comedies", with a happy ending) or unsuccessfully (in "tragedies", with an unhappy ending).

Without the second stage, there is no drama, no conflict. Without the first stage (the "setup"), there can be no second stage (the "upset"). And even though a few stories deliberately leave us "hanging" without a resolution (e.g., "The Lady, or the Tiger?"), most at least deal in some way with the conflict, either successfully (comedies) or unsuccessfully (tragedies).

In terms of a geographical image, the three stages are home, away, and back home again. The single most pervasive physical image for the protagonist's story is the road. Life is a road. In the profound words of Bilbo the Hobbit, "The Road goes ever on and on / Down from the door where it began. / Now far ahead the Road has gone / And I must follow, if I can, / Pursuing it with eager feet, / Until it joins some larger way / Where many paths and errands meet. / And whither then? I cannot say."

Sometimes the protagonist's journey brings him home literally, as with Ulysses, or with Frodo. But even then, "you can't go home again", to quote Thomas Wolfe's profound title, because even when home is the same, you are not. You can go back to your kindergarten classroom, but you no longer fit into its little seats. You are no longer one of the *Kinder*, and it is no longer a *Garten*. By God's severe mercy, Adam and Eve were banished from their Garden forever; and in the Bible's ambitious narrative of the whole of the human story, our end is *not* the same as our beginning: it is a city, not a garden. It is "east of Eden". It is resurrection, with Jesus, not simply resuscitation, as with Lazarus.

The theological terms for the three stages of this "theo-drama", or drama of God working in time, are "creation", "fall", and "redemption". But these are the stages not only of religion, but also of every story ever told. If the story is not created, there can be no drama because nothing can happen. If nothing in the story falls, again there is no drama because nothing needs to be changed. And if there is no possibility of either redemption or of damnation, again there is no drama because there is either no hope, if there is no redemption, or no fear, if there is no damnation.

The three stages may be called Life, Death, and Resurrection—not just of Christ, and not just of us, but of everything in time. (See Rom 8:18–23.) Whatever is born, must die—"whatever is an arising thing, that is also a setting thing", says Buddha. But because he denied the existence of the stronger-than-death soul or self, he did not know the one exception to that principle, and therefore he denied the third stage. His story is a two-act play rather than a three. Or, rather, it is a no-act play, for his "Nirvana", unlike the biblical Heaven, is not in any kind of time at all, not even redeemed and transformed time, but is totally timeless. It is the abolition rather than the transformation of time and ego, of both suffering and joy, and the abolition of both hate and love. I give Buddha one cheer, not two or three. But it is a very big one.

The only way to stage three, Resurrection, is through stage two, Death. As C. S. Lewis says, "We are like eggs at present. And you cannot go on indefinitely being just an ordinary, decent egg. We must be hatched or go bad." Hatching is like death to the egg, but it is the only way to real life. And if the "transhumanists" in Silicon Valley ever succeed in inventing artificial immortality by genetic engineering, they will create a world of rotten eggs that will never hatch, a Third Reich that actually *is* a "Thousand-Year Reich", a Hell on earth.

That seems to be close to the picture darkly suggested by Christ himself: that our future is not Utopian but Dystopian, in fact so bad that "if those days had not been shortened, no human being would be saved" (Mt 24:22). The last prayer we are given in Scripture, "*Maranatha!* Come, Lord Jesus", is equivalent to "Please shorten those days."

Resurrection is not simply the restoration of life over death, paradise regained over paradise lost.

The life of resurrection is a new *kind* of life: *zoe* rather than simply *bios*, supernatural rather than simply natural, divine rather than simply human. The human will be neither repeated nor abolished but transformed by the divine. Our destiny is *theosis*, divinization. That is not human theology but divine revelation (2 Pet 1:4), not mysticism but realism, not heresy but dogma, and not just Orthodoxy but orthodoxy. The three stages are not life, death, and life again; they are life, death, and resurrection. They are not happiness, misery, and happiness again; they are happiness, misery, and ecstasy.

The Trinitarian analogy is especially weak in this chapter, because "here" means "time", and the three Persons of the Trinity are not temporal, not stages; not first, second, and third in sequence. The Son is begotten of the Father eternally, and the Spirit proceeds eternally. So please do not seek an identification of one of these stages with the Father, one with the Son, and one with the Spirit. The same applies to time itself: no divine Person is past or future or even analogous to our past or future.

And even when we speak of some timeless and unchanging trinities, like the three kinds of goods and the corresponding three kinds of friendship in Aristotle, or the three levels of reality—what is superhuman, human, and subhuman, or God, Man, and Nature—or Heaven, Hell, and Purgatory, which are like the three possible grades for any test,

Pass, Fail, and Retest—here, too, there is no one-to-one correspondence with the three Persons of the Trinity, or none that I can see, anyway. There is, however, a correspondence with truth, goodness, and beauty, and also with life, light, and love, as we shall see in the next chapter.

The same remoteness from the divine Trinity is true of the cosmological trinities, or the trinities in the universe: matter, time, and space; matter, energy, and motion; past, present, and future; height, depth, and width. They do not correspond to the three divine Persons one to one. So let's not be literalistic, simple-minded, and fundamentalistic about the mysterious music that is God's creation and its varied relationships to him. To understand the divine creativity, let's be poets, not lawyers; musicians, not mathematicians.

Within the plot, and within the life of the protagonist, and sometimes of other characters, too, if they are treated with length and depth and breadth, we find the three stages of every story. They are stages of self-development, that is, of both self-discovery and of self-dying, of ego-dying. Thus they are all part of stage 2 in the larger narrative (life, *death*, resurrection). And this trinity is also found within a surrounding trinity: that of the three stages of any narrative or event: the beginning, the middle, and the end. They are the three stages of the middle stage, the three scenes of the second act. We are in "Middle-Earth" temporally as well as spatially.

Supernatural life (*zoe*) has three stages as does natural life (*bios*). As a plant has roots, shoots, and fruits, *zoe* has, first, justification, then sanctification, then glorification. And these three stages are accomplished especially (but not exclusively) by faith, hope, and charity, respectively. Love (charity) is the glory, the flower, or the fruit of the plant of supernatural life. Faith is its root, and hope is its growing shoot; that is why hope is the most time-centered of the theological virtues.

There are also three stages in religion, i.e., our relationship with God, both from our point of view and from God's point of view. From our point of view they are the three stages of evangelization; from God's point of view they are the three stages of revelation.

Our evangelization sometimes begins with truth and sometimes with goodness, but I think it usually begins with the love of beauty: the beauty of God, or of Christ, or of the saints, or of the theology, or of the liturgy, or of Christianity's high and holy morality, or of *agape* love. And this is the anonymous and ubiquitous presence of the Holy Spirit, drawing our spirit irresistibly (or resistibly: Calvin was wrong; if we have free will, grace is not irresistible). Even when evangelization into faith begins with truth or goodness (holiness), it is the *beauty* of truth or holiness that draws us. We have no defense or argument against beauty, as we have arguments against truth, and no temptation to ugliness, as we have temptations to moral evil. Beauty does not stand on the drawbridge and argue or fight for entrance to the castle; it seeps under the walls like water.

Evangelism is most effective when it begins with beauty and with the usually anonymous work of the Holy Spirit. It discovers the Trinity in reverse. In fact, we always discover God "in reverse", so to speak, that is, from effect to cause, from fingerprint to divine finger. For God has no cause, so we cannot move to God as from a cause to an effect but only from effects to their cause.

This movement to the First Cause has three aspects (the true, the good, and the beautiful), and even the theological (intellectual) and the moral (volitional) aspects of the Faith usually attract us first of all by their beauty. Beauty is the ambassador of the spirit, the point of the arrow.

Bishop Barron says: "The best evangelical strategy is one that moves from the beautiful to the good and finally to the true. Especially within our cultural matrix, so dominated by relativism [of both goodness and truth] ... commencing with either moral demand or the claim to truth will likely raise insuperable blocks in the person one wishes to evangelize.... But there is something unthreatening about the beautiful."

Our collective human history, like an individual human life, also has three stages from the viewpoint of God's intention in it, God's revelation of himself in it. The Bible is the story of that relationship. (Indeed, the very word "religion" means "binding-back relationship".) The Old Testament is the record of the revelation of God the Father; the Gospels, of Christ the Son; and the history of the Church, beginning with the Acts of the Apostles, of the Holy Spirit.

These are three stages of intimacy. God is love, and love's aim is intimacy, union. The Old Testament brings God intimately into our world from above; it reveals the God who stands infinitely above us yet who speaks to us. The Gospels reveal God closer, God beside us, God who became one of us, incarnate and human. God did this, as he does everything that he does, out of love, and love's demand for intimacy. Finally, even that is not intimate enough. Christ says it is better for us that he go away so that he can send the Spirit (Jn 16:7) because the Spirit is God within us, like a good haunting, a good possession. It is what is mocked by demon possession. God's possession perfects our freedom; demonic possession destroys it.

The spiritual life is also divided into three stages by most mystics: the purgative stage, the illuminative stage, and the unitive stage, which are also the stages of love and intimacy. However, these do not correspond exactly to the three theological virtues because all three virtues are presupposed and used in all three stages.

This structure is not limited to religion or the sacred; if the testimony of the saints is true, it is reflected in all character development. That is why secular psychologists often "crib" from the wisdom of religious mystics and saints: because it works!

Chapter Four

Why do our greatest *values* and themes come in threes?

We have explored three of the four dimensions of our story: the setting (the universe), the characters (ourselves), and the plot (our lives). The fourth and most important dimension is the theme, or the meaning, that is, the values, goals, ends, and purposes of the characters in the story.

The Greek word for this dimension is *telos*, so the knowledge or study (*logos*) of this *telos* is "teleology".

The primary reason modern Western man is bored, anxious, unhappy, and confused is that the prevailing philosophy of his culture tells him that there is no such thing as real teleology; that purposes and values are merely artificial subjective inventions of individual wills or of their cultures, not objective realities, so that our longing for them does not signify their reality—in other words that, as for Macbeth, life is "full of sound and fury [in pursuit of them, but] *signifying* nothing". According to our culture, the fact that we long for truth, goodness, and beauty does not mean, or "signify", their reality, because teleology is merely subjective, merely psychological. This is the meaning of "nihilism", or "nothing-ism". Obviously the setting (the universe) is not nothing, and the characters (ourselves) are not nothing, and the plot (the events of our lives) are not nothing, but our modern post-Christian, post-religious, and post-metaphysical culture has taught us that these themes or values in life are nothing, are not objective realities but merely our own artificial and arbitrary desires and dreams and inventions.

It is no accident that Nietzsche, the prophet of our culture, said that the only admirable figure he found in the entire New Testament was the only nihilist in those pages, namely, Pontius Pilate, whose philosophy was summarized in the ultimate cynicism, "What is truth?" Nietzsche called himself the first philosopher who questioned the "will to truth". He wrote: "Why truth? Why not rather untruth?"

There is no possible answer to that question. For "the true answer to your question" presupposes that very will to truth. Questioning the will to truth itself is the Devil's philosophy. It is spiritual suicide. It is the unforgivable sin, for if truth itself is refused, there is no possibility of salvation. Every operation needs light. A blind surgeon cannot heal anyone, much less himself.

THEME

This crisis of nihilism is the greatest, most fundamental crisis that the human race has ever faced, because no culture in history has ever survived without giving at least some answer to the question "What is the meaning of life?" What is its significance? What is its value? What is the end to which all our scientific technology and our social laws and reforms are means? What is the end of all ends, the *summum bonum*, or greatest good? If the question itself is refused, no answer can possibly be received. If the hand is not open, it cannot receive the gift.

What is the supreme good? What is the meaning of life? What is the object of our teleology? That was the question that every great philosopher, beginning with Socrates, Plato, and Aristotle, put at the very center of his philosophy, especially of his ethics, which is the division of philosophy that deals with the good. Our current crop of ethicists still ask questions about social and individual justice (how to treat each other) and sometimes (but only rarely) even about personal moral character, virtues, and vices, but they almost always ignore or avoid or declare meaningless and unanswerable the greatest question about the good, that is, the greatest ethical question of all: What is it all *for*? What is its end, or *telos*?

To use a memorable metaphor from C. S. Lewis, that omission is like a fleet of sailing ships getting only the lesser two-thirds of its sailing orders: directions on how to cooperate so that the ships of the fleet do not impede or ignore each other on their mission (social justice), and directions on how each ship is to stay shipshape and afloat (personal character), but no information at all on the most important question of all: Why are they there? Why are they sailing? What is their mission, both individual and social? Is it war, a pleasure cruise, a delivery of merchandise, a game, or a race?

In other words, this generation knows more than any other about almost everything (at least about everything that science and technology can master) but nothing at all about the most important of all questions: What is that everything for? Why do we live and exist at all? Why is life good and death bad? Never before has there been such a culture, the majority of whose mind-molders, both in formal and informal (media) education, increasingly teach this nihilism to the next generation. And that is the philosophy Western civilization is exporting, with increasing success, throughout the world. I cannot think of any more fundamental global disaster than that. It is toxic spiritual pollution.

So what *are* the values or themes of our human story? The three greatest values are, of course, truth, goodness, and beauty, "the true, the good, and the beautiful". Those are the three "themes" of the story of human life, both individually and collectively.

Different cultures "specialize in", concentrate on, focus on, or are famous for one or another of these values. In the Orient, India specializes in truth, especially as known by its mystics. China specializes in goodness, especially as recommended by its moralists, especially Confucius and Lao Tzu, in contrasting ways. Confucianism was the most long-lived and successful experiment in social harmony and social justice in all of human history, until it was replaced by its polar opposite, Communism, which is based on class conflict, tyranny, and totalitarianism disguised as egalitarianism. And Japan specializes in beauty, as created by its artists in many different media. In the West, to a less clear extent, Germany is famous for its philosophy and science, England for its practical laws, reconciling freedom and order, and France for its beauty, both of art and of cuisine: the world's greatest cathedrals and paintings and the world's best food.

Every individual, in all cultures, seeks truth, goodness, and beauty. And not just in a finite way, which would eventually get boring, but in an infinite way, so that an infinitely continuing Heaven would not ever get boring if it was the fulfillment of these three infinite desires.

All the characters in our story are fulfilled, happified, beatified, "flourished", by these three things.

The drama of the plot is always about getting or losing one or more of them. Even the setting is explained by them, for the setting is fitting *for that play*, that plot, those characters, and those themes.

Sometimes the three greatest values are identified as life (*zoe*), light (*phos*) or truth (*logos* or *aletheia*), and love (*agape*), e.g., by Saint John. In Hinduism, they are the three attributes of Brahman, the supreme reality: *sat* (infinite life, being, or power), *chit* (infinite understanding), and *ananda* (infinite joy through infinite love). Brahman is sometimes called *sat-chit-ananda*.

This is the life (*zoe*) of the Trinity: just as God's knowledge (*logos*) is so real that it is eternally begotten from the Father as a second Person, so God's love (*agape*) is so real that it eternally proceeds from Father and Son as a third Person. *Our* knowledge and love are choices and actions that are additions to our being, "accidents" added to our essence; God's knowledge and love *are* his being, his essence. This is God's Trinitarian life: being, or existence itself, is the essential nature of the Father, from whom proceeds both truth and love, as both light and heat proceed from the sun. The Son is Truth itself, the total self-knowledge and self-expression of the Father; and the Spirit is Love itself, the total self-giving of the Father and the Son to each other.

But these three (life, light, and love) do not correspond exactly to truth, goodness, *and beauty*, because beauty is not usually thought of as one of the three names for God (though it is for Augustine!), and life is not one of the three values we pursue infinitely (though we do long to live forever). The other two do correspond: truth corresponds to light, knowledge, or *logos*; and goodness corresponds to love.

This discrepancy between the two trinities of values (is it life, light, and love, or is it truth, goodness, and beauty?) does not invalidate the Trinitarian nature either of God or of our ultimate values, because life, or existence, is *the foundation* for the last two of the three *divine* attributes, while beauty is the *product* of the first two *human* values. Thus the discrepancy between the two trinities is accounted for by the two variables of (1) "foundation of" vs. (2) "product of" and (1) in God vs. (2) in us.

The *ultimate* reason truth, goodness, and beauty are our three highest values is founded in the divine Trinity, but the *immediate* reason for them is that they are the objects of our three distinctively human powers: mind, will, and heart. In other words, when we begin with God, we begin with existence or being or life or power, and then (not "then" in time, of course) comes the Son, the *Logos*, the Light, and then the Holy Spirit, the Love. But when we begin with man, we begin with truth and goodness and then note that beauty is also a uniquely human, spiritual, and infinite value as the

78   WHY DOES EVERYTHING COME IN THREES?

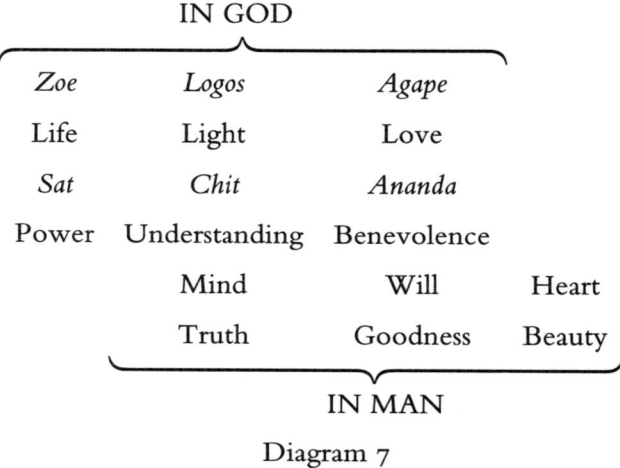

Diagram 7

child of truth and goodness. Being, life, or power is the ontological foundation of the other two, while beauty is their product.

❧

As truth is the object of the mind and goodness of the will, beauty is the object of the heart. "Heart" is a very complex term. It has many meanings. It can mean

1. whatever power loves in any way, with any kind of love, both distinctively human

loves and the loves that we share with the animals; or
2. the distinctively human power to appreciate and love beauty; or
3. the distinctively human power to will the good of another person; or
4. the distinctively human intellectual power of "intuition" as distinct from reasoning, calculating, or proving; or
5. all the distinctively human and spiritual emotions and feelings and sentiments that mere animals do not share, such as wonder, awe, gratitude, guilt, creative imagination, aesthetic appreciation, and the love that is a spontaneous feeling rather than a deliberately and freely chosen act of will; or
6. something quite mysterious and in fact indefinable: the pre-functional root of all these functions, the source of all these powers; the person who has them and exercises them; the non-objectified and non-objectifiable and non-definable "I" who "has" or "owns" all these powers (after all, we speak of "my" mind and "my" choices and "my" loves) and who also "owns" or "has" a body ("my" body) and a soul ("my" soul); the single "I" that unifies both body and soul (or body, soul, and spirit) and, within the soul, all its powers and actions.

To keep things relatively simple and clear here, let's use "heart" in meaning no. 5, the distinctively human emotions, the spiritual emotions, the emotions that are "intentional", i.e., that intend, mean, refer to, point to, signify, or are based on the understanding of something outside themselves. Animal emotions signify only states inside themselves. They do not reach out toward biologically and physically unattainable and transcendent objects like truth and goodness and beauty. Platypuses are not philosophers, and monkeys are not moralists, and armadillos are not artists.

However, "heart" in the most basic and mysterious sense of the personal center that "has" all these powers and attributes ("heart" in sense no. 6 above) is involved in all three of the distinctively human values; in truth and goodness as well as beauty. When we speak of the intellect, we speak of the "heart" as that which intuits or "just sees" intellectually. That is sense no. 4 above. When we speak of the will, we speak of the "heart" as that which knowingly chooses to love the best good of the other. That is sense no. 3 above. Kant simply called the will the "practical reason". When we speak of the emotions, we speak of the "heart" as that which feels and emotes. That is sense no. 5 above.

We love truth, goodness, and beauty because our three main human powers are the mind, the will, and the heart; and truth, goodness, and beauty are the food of these three stomachs, the quenching of these three thirsts. The mind, the will, and the heart are, respectively, the sources of thinking, of choosing, and of feeling. Truth is the object of the mind, goodness is the object of the will, and beauty is the object of the heart.

The three "theological virtues" of faith, charity, and hope correspond to these three powers (mind, will, and heart) as they relate to supernatural objects: to three attributes of God and, thus, ultimately to a single supernatural object, the one God.

Faith means believing that everything God reveals is *true*. ("What God reveals" supernaturally is the Bible and, for Catholics and Orthodox, the Church's Sacred Apostolic Tradition, summarized in the Creeds.)

Charity means loving as God loves and willing what God wills. ("What God wills" is summarized in the Commandments.)

Hope means desiring and aspiring after what he promises. ("What God promises" and what we should desire is summarized in the Lord's Prayer.)

Saint Thomas says that the whole Christian religion is contained in these three things, the Creed, the Commandments, and the Lord's Prayer.

The three supreme values, like the three Persons of the Trinity, are one. They are not one in their essential nature and definition, for truth is a mental object, goodness is a volitional object, and beauty is an affective object. But they are one in another way: they are inclusive of each other. Truth is in itself good and beautiful; goodness is in itself true and beautiful, and beauty is in itself true and good.

Truth may sometimes seem evil and ugly, but it never is. A particular truth may be evil (e.g., "You are going to Hell") or ugly (e.g., "Your intestines are falling into the mud"), but truth *as such* is good. In fact it is an absolute good, not good only relative to or justified by anything else. It is good for itself, by itself. That is one of the greatest differences between the medieval mind and the modern Baconian, Utilitarian mind, which sees truth as a means to power or pleasure rather than as an end in itself and self-justifying.

A particular truth may be bad for us, e.g., knowing secrets that it is better for us not to know. Many truths are also ugly, either aesthetically (e.g., vomit) or morally (e.g., war). But truth is like light: in itself it is good and beautiful, even though it reveals many things that are not. When light shines on garbage, it is still light and still beautiful. *It* is not garbage.

Good may seem sometimes untrue (e.g., apparently unattainable ideals), but goodness itself is not. In fact, "that's too good to be true" is always in some way false unless God does not exist. The good is our true end, our true meaning, our true happiness, and our true identity.

Beauty may seem untrue (e.g., when a beautiful costume or makeup is removed from an ugly person) or bad for us (e.g., any thing or person that tempts us by its beauty to do something wicked); but that is not beauty's fault. Just as "all truth is God's truth" (Arthur Holmes) and all goodness is God's goodness, all authentic beauty is God's beauty, "patches of Godlight" (C. S. Lewis) in our dark woods.

Within the true, we have more trinities, for instance, the three acts of the mind in traditional logic and also the psychological trinity of the subject (the knower), the object (the known), and the relationship (the knowing).

Within the good, we also have more trinities, such as Plato's distinction between things that are good only as means (like money), things that are good only as ends (like the contemplation of truth), and things that are good both as means and as ends (like health or justice). We also have the psychological trinity of the subjective will's desire for the good, the objective good desired, and the relation between them, the act that unites them.

Beauty also has a Trinitarian structure, both psychologically and ontologically. Ontologically, Saint Thomas says that beauty has three properties: clarity, proportion, and brightness or radiance.

Psychologically, there is the appreciation of beauty, the beauty appreciated, and the relationship or act that unites them.

❧

The fact that goodness has many trinities is clear when we look at its opposite, evil.

The three greatest evils are (1) pride, (2) greed, and (3) lust.

(1) Pride seeks power, (2) greed seeks money (and the things money can buy), and (3) lust seeks pleasure (especially sexual pleasure). Power, money, and sex are the three things we fight over the most.

Temptations to evil come from three sources, "the world, the flesh, and the Devil". (1) Pride comes from the Devil, (2) greed comes from the world, and (3) lust comes from the flesh.

("The flesh", by the way, does not mean the body but the fallen human self as a whole, especially the fallen, selfish hopes and desires that are in the soul. The biblical terms for body and soul are *soma* and *psyche*. The biblical terms for the fallen self and the redeemed self are *sarx* and *pneuma*, or "flesh" and "spirit", i.e., the human spirit lived in by the Holy Spirit.)

Christ's three temptations in the wilderness were (1) to worship the *Devil* (because the Devil would give him the whole world—not the world of power and politics, which would not tempt even a reasonably good sinner, but the whole world of souls that he had in Hell—a real temptation to the lover and Savior of souls!); (2) to win the *world* by spectacular miracles like jumping off the temple roof; and (3) to succumb to the desires of the *flesh* by breaking his fast and turning stones into bread.

(1) The Devil is our false God; (2) the world is our false home; and (3) the flesh is our false self.

We are to (1) worship God alone, (2) use the things of the world, and (3) love and respect ourselves and each other as ends, as intrinsic goods. We are tempted (1) to use God or each other, (2) to worship the world or ourselves, and either (3a) to love the world more than we love ourselves and our neighbor or (3b) to love God less than we love ourselves and our neighbor.

Our weapons against these three evils are the three monastic vows of (1) poverty, (2) obedience, and (3) chastity.

These weapons are also forms of the three theological virtues of (1) faith, (2) hope, and (3) charity.

1. Faith trusts God and therefore unclutches its hand and does not greedily try to win the things in the world to overcome poverty. The virtue of voluntary poverty, or poverty of spirit, tests our faith and humbles our greed. Christ and the saints declared it "blessed".

2. Hope avoids both presumption, which is pride, and despair, which is also pride but in a disguised form. The virtue of obedience tests our humility and humbles our pride.

3. And charity, or true love, overcomes lust, or false love. The virtue of chastity tests our charity and humbles our lust.

Faith, hope, and charity are also ultimately one, like the three Persons of the Trinity. You can see this unity when you look at the eyes of a baby in its mother's arms looking up into its mother's face and smiling. "Out of the mouths of babes" can come deep wisdom.

Chapter Five

Why does the One God come in three Persons?

Obviously, the ultimate reason for all the trinities we have seen in many aspects of God's creation is the fact that the Creator is a Trinity. Creation always reveals the creator; art reveals the artist. The medievals liked to say that God wrote two books: nature and Scripture.

But why is God himself a Trinity?

The reason for that cannot be extrinsic but must be intrinsic. The reason for trinities in everything except God is God himself, who is extrinsic or transcendent to the whole of creation, or nature; but the reason God himself is a Trinity is intrinsic, in God himself. In other words, God is the reason for himself as well as the reason for everything else. Nothing else can be the reason for God. (We can give reasons for *believing in* God's existence, but those are not reasons for God's *existence*. The effect is not the reason for the being of the cause; the cause is the reason for the being of the effect. Our *knowledge* of the effect is the reason for our *knowledge* of the cause. In other words, while reality always moves forward, our thought usually moves backward, not forward, except when it predicts.)

God's essence is existence. He does not "have" existence or "get" existence from any cause; he *is* existence by his own essence. That is why he can give existence to everything else, which is what is meant by "creating" it. Everything else, every being, is dependent on him for everything it is; he is not dependent on anything.

He is not *a* being, one of many, but Being itself, or rather Being himself. His own self-revelation and name is I AM (Ex 3:14). He is the union, or rather the identity, of "I" (personhood) and "AM" (Being). For Being at its height, in its perfection, when not limited or restricted in any way, is personal, not impersonal; subject, not just object; "I AM", not just "It is."

And now comes the ultimate answer to the ultimate question. The reason God is a Trinity is because God is love, true love, total love, complete love, self-giving love, altruistic love, *agape* love of the other.

Love of self, self-love, may be good, but it is not altruistic love, which means love of the other. In order to be not just a lover but love itself, in himself, in order to be complete love, God must include otherness in himself. Thus he must be more than only one Person. Without otherness, love cannot be altruistic. "Altruism" comes from "alter", which means "other".

God lacks nothing. He does not need us or the world. Therefore his love is not needy, it is not the desire for something he does not have. It is not *eros*, which means the desire for some absent good. No good is lacking or absent in God.

And if God is complete in himself, and thus his love is altruistic not egotistic, then the only possible motive for him to create us and the world must be altruistic, not egotistic. We and our world have been loved into existence.

It is for our glory, not his, that he created us and our world. When he asks for our adoration and worship, it is not to increase his good (that is impossible) but to increase ours. He does not need us; we need him, and we need to know and express our need for him.

Thus the purpose of prayer is not to change God's mind or will, to conform his will to ours, but to fulfill it, to conform our will to his. God is perfect and complete in himself in every possible way. He cannot be changed, either for the better or for the worse. That is impossible. And we should not try to do the impossible.

God is complete love: lover, loved, and loving. Not just a lover. If God was not love itself but only a lover, a single Person, then he could only be a selfish lover until he created other beings to love. He would need us in order to be an unselfish lover, an *agape* lover instead of an *eros* lover. But that is impossible: How could God's own perfection, in fact, his highest perfection, depend on us?

Agape is greater than *eros*, so God, the most perfect Being, must be *agape*, not *eros*. And *agape* requires otherness. Therefore divine perfection requires otherness, or plurality. Plurality as well as unity must be in God's eternal essence.

Now we are going to do some metaphysics. Metaphysics is the division of philosophy that deals with being itself, or existence itself. It is the most difficult, most abstract, and most ultimate kind of thought. Yet everyone can understand at least some of it, some of its basic and most important truths. Here is one of them:

The fact that God is a Trinity and that God is love (which two statements say the same thing, or at least necessarily imply each other) is tightly connected with—no, is *necessarily* connected with—the fact that God is infinite existence (Being) itself rather than *a* being, a being with a limiting essence. If God were *a* being, he would be finite and limited by other beings. God is not *a* being, even the greatest of beings, but Being itself, infinite and unrestricted.

But that does not mean that God is an abstraction, like redness itself or twoness itself or justice itself. Those are all essences. They do not exist as entities, beings, substances, things. They are the natures of things, the attributes of things, the properties of things. They are adjectives, not nouns. Adjectives modify nouns. They do not exist all by themselves but only as the attributes of nouns. Adjectives are relative to nouns; nouns are not relative to adjectives. Nouns express what Aristotle called "substances", and adjectives express what he called "accidents" or properties or attributes.

Essences are finite. They are limits on existence. They are like the banks of a river or the borders of a country. God's essence is existence itself, infinite and unlimited and complete and perfect existence, the fullness of existence, the fullness of being. (Remember, existence is not an abstract fact but a concrete act or actuality. God is not an abstraction!)

Essences are relative to existence; they are potentialities for existence. Redness is one of the colors material things can have. Justice is one of the virtues individuals or societies can have. Essences (like adjectives) are not ontologically absolute, not beings in themselves, but relative to the things (nouns) that have them. But existence itself is absolute.

Existence is not an abstraction. It is not just a fact but an act. It is not necessarily a temporal, changing *activity* (what Aquinas called "second act", or the second meaning of the word "act"), but it is an *actuality* (what Aquinas called "first act").

First act (the act of existence, the actuality of existence) always expresses itself in second act (activity); actualities always act in some way, make their presence known, make a difference to something else. Even a stone that does not move occupies space and keeps other material objects from being in that space. A large rock can block your way to go in or out of a gate, and that might be a very important activity even though it is not a movement, a change. It might save your life or kill you.

Essences are potentialities for existence. Triangularity is a potentiality for a building, for instance: a teepee or a pyramid, a way the building can be shaped and take up space, a way it can be.

That "God is existence itself" and that "God is love" are two truths that say virtually the same thing. At least they imply each other, even though to our mistaken minds they may seem in contrast, for two reasons: first, we mistakenly think of existence as being simply the abstract fact that things exist, rather than the dynamic act of existing, and second, because we mistakenly think of love as a mere feeling or desire (*eros*). But existence is an act, not a fact; and love is self-giving, not self-aggrandizement.

Complete love requires (1) a lover, (2) a beloved, and (3) an act of loving. They are (1) the giver, (2) the gift, and (3) the giving. They are also (1) the self,

(2) the other, and (3) the relationship between them. Thus the Father is (1) the absolute origin, the Son is (2) the absolute object, and the Spirit is (3) the absolute relationship or activity or eternal process of being and knowing and loving, which is what God is. The Father is Being and the source of all being; the Son is the Father's perfect self-knowledge; and the Spirit is the perfect love between Father and Son. The Father's knowledge is so perfect that it is (eternally) another Person, "begotten" like a Son; and the love between Father and Son is so perfect that it is (eternally) another Person, "proceeding" from the Father and the Son.

If we omit the divinely revealed names of "Father", "Son", and "Spirit", that is the *philosophical* explanation and argument for the Trinity. Philosophical arguments are based on and justified by reason alone. They do not presuppose religious faith or divine revelation.

Theological arguments do presuppose religious faith. That is why they tell us more, and that is also why they convince fewer people, since not everyone has religious faith. Here is the *theological* argument for the Trinity. It is based on the data of divine revelation in Scripture.

1. First of all, it is clear that there is only one God, one real God, one true God. Thus the very first commandment is to worship only the one true

God. This is repeated hundreds of times in the Old Testament. The primary prayer in Judaism is the *shema*: "Hear, O Israel: the LORD our God is one LORD; and you shall love the LORD your God with all your heart, and with all your soul, and with all your might" (Deut 6:4–5).

2. The Being Jesus calls his Father is God. "God" is the proper name for this divine Person, who tells Moses his own essential and eternal name when he says: "I AM" (Ex 3:14).

3. Jesus calls himself the Son of God. The Son of God is also God, for just as the son of a human is a human person and the son of a Martian is a Martian person, so the Son of God is a divine Person. The Son of God is God. (The word "God" can designate either a single Person, the Father, or the one God.)

There are dozens of ways in all four Gospels in which Jesus both claims and shows that he is divine and not merely human.

The first, most nonnegotiable, most distinctive, and most foundational truth of Christianity, expressed in what was probably the very first Christian creed, one that contained only four words, is the formula: "Jesus Christ is Lord" (Phil 2:11). Christians, like Jews, did not call Caesar or any other creature "Lord" in an absolute sense. That was why Christians and Jews were the only two religious groups Rome persecuted. Like modern Western "liberalism" or "progressivism", Rome was very tolerant and ecumenical except when it came to "exclusive" and demanding truth-claims.

4. The Holy Spirit is God, is divine. That is also clear from many Scripture passages. And he is a Person, for we can "grieve" him (Eph 4:30).

5. But the Father, the Son, and the Spirit are not the same Person. They are three different Persons. They have relations of love and knowing with each other. The Son conforms his mind and will to the Father, and they send their Spirit by an act of will.

To use the language of science, the doctrine of the Trinity is the only hypothesis that accounts for and explains all of this fivefold data. Hypotheses are tested and confirmed by data. Divinely revealed data are supernatural and non-empirical data, but they are data.

The doctrine of the Trinity at first seems to be self-contradictory, for since three is not one and one is not three, how can anything be both one and three? But the Trinity is not a self-contradiction (that would make it not only impossible but meaningless) because although nothing can be both one and three in the same way, it can be one in one way and three in another way. It would be a self-contradiction to say that God was both one person and also three persons. And it would be a self-contradiction to say that God was one being or substance or had one nature or essence and also was three beings or substances or had three essences or natures. But the dogma ("dogma" simply means "data", "that which is given to us") of the Trinity does not say either of those two things. It says that God is three Persons, not just one, and that he has one essential nature or essence (his essence is existence itself), not three; that he is one Being, not three.

He is one God in three Persons. The whole God is each Person. Thus it is more correct to say that God is one God "in" three Persons than to say that God is three Persons "in" one God, since the latter sounds like God has or contains three parts. God has no parts. He is absolutely one. Each Person IS the single God, who is not a "whole" composed of parts.

The Christian Creed that states the dogma of the Trinity most completely is the Creed of Saint Athanasius. To my mind, this is a strikingly clear piece of evidence that when you enter the Catholic faith, you do not bow down and creep into a narrow, dark little cave and recite a narrow, dark little set of platitudes—which is how the world sees it—but exactly the opposite: you emerge from a narrow, dark little cave into a cathedral that is more comprehensive than the cosmos, with the lightning and thunder of Heaven playing triumphant music around your gloriously defenseless head. The Church is the deeper meaning of the allegory of

Plato's Cave. The real "cave men" are the secular "progressives" who stubbornly stick to the conservatism of their little cave and call themselves "liberals" and who call those who are liberated from the cave of mere matter and appearances into the wild weather of Heaven "conservatives".

The statements of the Athanasian Creed are highly theological, theoretical, or contemplative; but the context of the Creed's statements about the Trinity is the most practical thing in the world: our salvation. The point of the Creed is that to be saved is to be saved *by this God*. The Creed describes the God who saves us, the God who is our whole hope.

It makes many startling and strange statements about God, in describing him, but it does not claim to define him. We can define only the finite. To define is to limit, to circumscribe. We can't even define ourselves as persons, as "I's"; how could we define God? We can't define our own finite "I"; how could we define God's infinite "I"?

When the Creed says that one must believe this if one is to be saved, it does not mean that those who are honestly mistaken and do not believe all these things will go to Hell. Its last line, "This is the Catholic [universal] faith: unless *each* [one] has believed it faithfully and firmly, he will not be saved" does not mean to judge *individuals* but *ideas*. To be intolerant of wrong ideas is not necessarily to be intolerant to the people who hold them. We are not admitted to Heaven only if we pass a theology exam! But we are admitted to Heaven by *this God*, whether we fully understand that or not.

Here is the meat of the Athanasian Creed:

> This, then, is the Catholic faith: We worship one God in the Trinity and the Trinity in the unity, without confusing the Persons or separating the substance; for indeed the Person of the Father is one, [the Person] of the Son another, [the Person] of the Holy Spirit another; but the divinity of the Father, the Son, and the Holy Spirit is one: [their] glory equal, and [their] majesty coeternal.
>
> As the Father is, so is the Son, [and] so is the Holy Spirit: uncreated the Father, uncreated the Son, uncreated the Holy Spirit; infinite the Father, infinite the Son, infinite the Holy Spirit; eternal the Father, eternal the Son, eternal the Holy Spirit; and yet [they are] not three eternal beings, but one eternal; just as [they are] not three uncreated beings or three infinite beings, but one *uncreated* [infinite] and one *infinite* [uncreated] being. In like manner, omnipotent [is] the Father, omnipotent the Son, omnipotent the Holy Spirit; and yet [they are] not three omnipotent beings but one omnipotent being. Therefore, the Father [is] God, the Son [is] God, the Holy Spirit [is] God; and yet [there are] not three Gods but one God. In the same way, the Father [is] Lord, the Son [is]

Lord, the Holy Spirit [is] Lord; yet [there are] not three Lords, but there *is* one Lord; for just as we are compelled by Christian truth to confess each Person individually as God and Lord, just so the Catholic religion forbids us to say that there are three Gods or three Lords.

The Father was not made by anyone; nor was he created or begotten; the Son is from the Father alone, neither made nor created but generated [begotten]; the Holy Spirit [is] from the Father and the Son, neither made nor created nor generated, but proceeding. Therefore, [there is] one Father, not three Fathers; one Son, not three Sons; one Holy Spirit, not three Holy Spirits. And in this Trinity, [there is] nothing before or after, nothing greater or lesser, but all three Persons are coequal and coeternal with each other. And so, in all things, as was said already above, both the *unity in the Trinity and the Trinity in the unity* [the Trinity in the unity and the unity in the Trinity] must be worshipped. (DZ 75)

Except for their *relationships* to each other, each of the three divine Persons is all that the two others are: infinite life, light, and love; being, truth, and goodness.

Thus Christ is the fullness of all three. He says, "I am the way, and the truth, and the life" (Jn 14:6).

"The way" is not just a set of guidelines but the Way of *agape* love. Love is the Way, the way we are to live, the way God lives, the way God *exists*. That is the life, the actuality, the existence, the being of God. It is not an abstraction; it is a divine Person. *Agape* love is the Holy Spirit.

"The Truth" is not just correct thoughts but the *Logos*, the Word of the Father. *Logos* is an incredibly rich word in Greek, but its three fundamental meanings are: intelligible being or truth; understanding or knowledge of being or truth; and revelation, speech, communication, or word expressing that knowledge or understanding.

Christ the *Logos* does not merely *teach* the truth, he *is* the Truth. Truth is identified in a special, though not exclusive, way with the Son. Truth, like life, or being, is not an abstraction but a divine Person! "Jesus" (meaning "Savior" or "God saves") is his human name and task.

And "the Life" is eternal existence itself, the infinite power to be and to give being. This, too, is not an abstraction but a divine Person. When he reveals his own essential and eternal name to Moses in the Burning Bush, that name is so holy that no Jew will ever pronounce it. It is "I AM", the union of Being and Person, "is-ness" and "I-ness".

From a higher point of view, from God's side of the prism, the Trinity is one of Being (or Life), Truth, and Goodness. Beauty is often called the child of the marriage of Truth and Goodness, a little like the next generation of the family. (It is a mere and remote analogy, but a real one.) From our point of view here on the finite side of the prism of creation, the Trinity is one of Goodness, Truth, and Beauty.

Thus from this higher point of view, the "Life" in the Trinity of life, light, and love is Being itself, existence, actuality, which underlies absolutely everything, and this is associated especially with the Father. Light or Truth is associated especially with the Son, the *Logos*. And Love is associated especially with the Spirit, who is the love between the Father and the Son. (See Diagram 7 for an explanation of why these two trinities do not contradict each other even though they do not match one to one.)

Truth and goodness are always two of the three. In our great epics, there is always a prophet or wizard and a king or ruler. The third character, the priestly one, is less clear, as is the third human power, the heart, and as is beauty as compared with truth and goodness.

Sometimes the third character's value in our epics is more like power or life or Being, which is *before* truth and goodness, and sometimes it is more like the child, the humble servant or priest. The "bottom line" is that whether Being is added before the other two (truth and goodness) or Beauty is added afterward, there are always three.

There is also a trinity *within* the *Logos*. Being, seeing, and saying are the three meanings of *logos*: intelligibility, intelligence, and communication. Philosophically, the study of being is metaphysics, the study of knowing or truth is epistemology, and the study of words or language or communication is linguistics. This trinity begins with being, or life, so it does not include beauty as one of its three, but it produces beauty as its "extra" child.

Seeing, saying, and *singing* (exulting, glorifying, praising) are also sometimes said to be the three meanings of *logos*, and they correspond to mind, will, and heart, and thus to truth, goodness, and beauty.

৵

The most remarkable thing about the Trinity is not the threeness, and not the oneness, but the oneness of the threeness with the oneness.

৵

A word about the most practical and important of these three values, namely, love.

"God IS love" means that love (*agape*) is God's very being (*esse*) and life (*zoe*).

The consequence of this abstract-sounding principle is that in us love is not merely the best thing the soul can *do*, but it is the very life (*zoe*) of the soul, a reflection of how love is the very life or being or essence or nature of God.

The alternatives to love are hate and indifference, and since love is the very life of the soul, hate kills souls and indifference lets souls die.

Truth is as absolute and nonnegotiable as love.

Love and truth are ultimately one, for love is also the light (*phos*) and truth (*logos, aletheia*) of the soul. Love is even "the *only* truth", in the sense that love is the only way truly to know other people. It is the very eye of the soul. ("The heart has its reasons that reason [alone] does not know.") Simple saints understand other persons more truly and profoundly than the most brilliant philosophers and psychologists.

The fact that life, light, and love, or being, knowing, and loving, are not merely abstractions, and not even merely actions, but divine Persons is so remarkable that it is almost unthinkable. It is like saying that the meaning of life said hello to me today. Saint Paul often shows us that what to us are abstractions are really concrete persons, as when he says that Christ does not merely *give* us wisdom but that he *is* "our wisdom, our righteousness and sanctification and redemption" (1 Cor 1:30) because the Father has "made him to be" these things. In the New Testament, abstractions often leap into life like a jack in the box! And in the Old Testament, too, where Eternal Existence Itself speaks to Moses and says "I AM".

Truth is a Person: "I AM the Truth."

Goodness is a Person: "I AM the Way."

Existence, or Life, is a Person: "I AM the Life." "I AM WHO AM." Being is a "who", not a "what".

Do I comprehend this? Certainly not. But I apprehend it, because it is revealed to us by God through Christ and his Church and her Scriptures. We can apprehend the incomprehensible.

God always amazes us. Everyone who ever met Jesus is described by some form of the word "*thaumadzein*", amazement, wonder, astonishment, shock: his enemies, his friends, and agnostics who went away shaking their heads and saying "No man ever spoke like this man" (Jn 7:46). "The crowds were astonished at his teaching, for he taught them as one who had authority, and not as their scribes" (Mt 7:28–29). If it does not amaze and discombobulate and turn you upside down (that is, really right side up), it is not God. If you can understand it, it is not God. If it is what you expected, it is not God. The very last thing I want to do in this book is to make the Trinity tame and expected and domesticated. The supreme manifestation of God was what Blake called "Christ the Tiger", not Christ the kitten.

Chapter Six

The practical "payoff": What difference does it make?

William James, one of the most commonsensical and non-ideologized of all philosophers, goes so far as to say that if an idea makes no difference to us, to our actual lived life, to our experience; if its truth and falsehood are equally non-impactful; then for all practical purposes, it is neither true nor false for us. This is not a subjectivism or relativism, though perhaps it confuses "truth" with "meaning". It is essentially the principle Jesus stated when he said, "By their fruits you shall know them." He was speaking of *people*, but the principle applies to *ideas*, too. As Richard Weaver said in his memorable title, "Ideas Have Consequences".

James gave the amusing example of two philosophers who thought they were arguing about what was happening when a man and a squirrel chased each other around the same tree trunk, neither one ever catching, or catching up to, the other. What the two philosophers argued about was whether the man and the squirrel circumambulated each other or the tree or both? After presenting their contrary arguments, each of the two philosophers called the other a stupid idiot and stormed off in protest. It was, to James, an image of much of the history of Western philosophy.

An example of similar truthlessness or meaninglessness, given by G. E. Moore, who was another rare defender of common sense, was Kant's and Hegel's view that time and space were not really real, not "noumenal", but only "phenomenal". Moore proposed judging this view by the "silly question" technique: ask the question the little boy in "The Emperor's New Clothes" would have asked: "Does that mean that I didn't really eat my lunch after I ate my breakfast, or that an elephant isn't really bigger than a mouse?" If so, it's insane. If not, it's only a technical and confusing way to say what we all know is true: that we *did* eat lunch after breakfast and that elephants *are* bigger than mice. If it makes no difference, except in words, then we should say to it what Rhett Butler said so frankly to Scarlett O'Hara in *Gone with the Wind*.

In this final chapter, I want to apply this principle to the idea of the Trinity. I want to ask what difference it makes to our lives.

And my answer is that it makes a total difference to everything.

First of all, it makes a difference to our religious life, that is, our relation to God. We naturally tend to think that while God is the *object* of our prayer, nevertheless our own souls, our own hearts and minds and wills, are the *origin* and motivation or moving power from inside ourselves, so to speak, of our prayer. And we also tend to think that our words and techniques are the highway or road or path or method or *way* we as human subjects relate to God as our religious object. The Trinity makes two important corrections to that natural assumption, and both are shocking but helpful blows to our pride and good reasons for humility. As C. S. Lewis puts it,

> An ordinary simple Christian kneels down to say his prayers. He is trying to get into touch with God. But if he is a Christian he knows that what is prompting him to pray is also God: God, so to speak, inside him. But he also knows that all his real knowledge of God comes through Christ, the Man who was God—that Christ is standing beside him, helping him to pray, praying for him. You see what is happening. God is the thing to which he is praying—the goal he is trying to reach. God is also the thing inside him which is pushing him

on—the motive power. God is also the road or bridge along which he is being pushed to that goal. So that the whole threefold life of the three-personal Being is actually going on in that ordinary little bedroom where an ordinary man is saying his prayers.

God the Father is the ultimate object of all prayer and even of all effort and aspiration and good desire, whether consciously or unconsciously. God the Holy Spirit is the ultimate subject, the divine Person who moves the human person to pray (not by removing his free will but by enlivening it and using it and perfecting it). God the Son is the way, the road, the relationship, the vehicle by which this human subject and this divine object are connected. He is the universal mediator: "No one comes to the Father, but by me" (Jn 14:6).

This fact of the divine priority in all three dimensions, the fact that God is the ultimate First Cause and the Final End and also the Way for everything good, both in creation and in our salvation and our motivation—this fact, like all facts, can be misused and twisted, as it is by those who deny human free will and responsibility and say "Well, if God has to be the First Cause of my prayer, then I can't be the First Cause, so I'm not going to start anything, I'll just wait for God to act on me."

The mistake there is both intellectual and moral.

The intellectual mistake is not understanding that God's will turns our wills on, not off; that God's causality and ours are not rivals but co-operators, operators or workers together; that divine grace perfects nature and human nature, rather than bypassing it or demeaning it.

The moral mistake is to pretend not to know what we cannot *not* know by our own conscience, which is God's prophetic voice in our soul: that our obligation is not first of all to understand but first of all to obey. "Pray" is not an idea or an ideal or a suggestion; it is a commandment. First, we do it; then, we begin to understand it. We do not first understand how digestion works and, only then, eat and, thus, survive. We first eat and, therefore, survive and, only then, gradually come to understand how eating and digestion work.

This is especially true in our relationship with other persons. Only if we first love them will we deeply understand them. As the Orthodox love to remind us, "Orthopraxy (right practice) leads to orthodoxy (right belief)." Your super-intelligent psychiatrist who does not love you knows (*wissen, savoir*) many *truths about* you that your best friend does not know; but your best friend, who truly loves you even though he is not super-intelligent, knows (*kennen, connaître*) you far better than your psychiatrist does.

Jesus uses this principle as his fundamental answer to the hermeneutical question, the question of interpretation. How are we to understand and interpret his teachings? And how can we know that they are from God, whom he calls his Father? In the seventh chapter of John's Gospel, the Jews who did not believe in him ask Jesus that double question. And Jesus' answer is startling and discombobulating to us who want an escape clause: "If any man's will is to do his [the Father's] will, he shall know whether the teaching is from God" (Jn 7:17). That principle is worth more than all the books on hermeneutics in all the libraries in the world.

When it comes to persons, as distinct from science, love is the key to understanding. And God is love because God is a Trinity: not just a lover, but complete Love Itself. So the Trinity is not only the foundation of Christian *theology* but also the foundation of Christian *morality*, the morality of love. Love "goes all the way up" into absolute, ultimate, eternal Reality. It is the very life of the Trinitarian God. *That* is why it is absolute and nonnegotiable for us. For, as God said many times to his chosen people, giving them the ultimate metaphysical reason for the morality of "be a saint", "You must be holy for I the Lord your God am holy."

That meant two things: that we must be holy *as* God is holy, i.e., in the same way that God is holy, that is, by loving; and also that we must be thus holy *because* God is thus holy: we must conform to the essential nature of absolute reality. We must live in the real world, not in any of the idolatrous worlds of our own fallen, foolish, and fickle, sinful, shallow, and selfish imagination, dreams, and desires.

Prayer is the primary way of doing that. It is essentially the recognition of reality, the reality that God is here and that God is the Main Thing, the Main Fact. Prayer is essentially sanity, the sanity of living in the real world, which means living in the presence of That Which Is Really Here. Prayer is how to live in the real world. We acknowledge the big, beautiful elephant in the middle of our living room. We treat God as present, not absent. Prayer is essentially what Brother Lawrence called "the practice of the presence of God". And we should be learning increasingly to "pray constantly" (1 Thess 5:17).

Here is a tiny practical suggestion about one easy and delightful way to pray in a Trinitarian way.

Methods, or "ways", of praying are far less important than we think—so say all the saints—but some can be helpful. Here is a very simple and concrete one that I have found useful, and it is based on God being the trinity-in-unity of life (being), light (truth), and love (charity).

Unless you are physically or psychologically allergic to sunlight, just go sit in the warm sun for a few minutes and deliberately accept its rays as gifts from

God. Remember that God created everything in the universe *for us*, for our instruction and edification and ultimate happiness, for our closer relationship to him. Everything is an icon, a holy picture or symbol or image, as a part of the great cathedral that is the universe. (Some of the icons are gargoyles!) And the sun is perhaps the most obvious of all icons and, thus, often idolatrously worshipped by pagans. It is not God, of course, but is a great gift of God, a present really presented in the present. It looks very glorious, and it feels very good. It is a natural symbol of the brilliance of God's light and the warmth of his love. And it is real, not an abstract idea.

The sun gives us three things, at once and immediately. And they are the three Trinitarian values we have seen in the last chapter: life (actuality, existence, reality, being), light (knowledge, understanding, truth), and love (*agape*, goodwill).

First of all, the sun gives us life or actual being. It is most obviously real and makes a difference to everything in this world. It is not imaginary, not subjective, not an idea or an ideal, not a thought or an abstraction, a law or a principle. It is totally nonideological. It announces its existence very loudly throughout the whole atmosphere, the dome of heaven.

Finite being is like the atmosphere God gave us to filter his infinite being, which we could not otherwise endure. As the physical atmosphere filters the sun's rays, the atmosphere of the finite universe brings God's infinite Being to us in finite and endurable shreds and shards. Finitude is our ontological filter.

The atmosphere is to the sun also somewhat similar to what our bodies are to our souls: a finitizing. Our souls are not actually infinite, of course—only God is—but they are potentially infinite, like the series of positive numbers, unlimited in potential for more, for knowing more and loving more, though never actually infinite. They are also potentially infinite in relation to the rest of the universe, since we can in principle eventually know any and all finite things. As Aristotle says, "the soul is potentially all things", i.e., it can contain mentally anything, the forms or natures or ideas of anything in the universe.

The body is the image or analogy for the spiritual soul. Asked what a human soul looked like, Wittgenstein replied, "like a human body". That is why we can speak (analogically but truly) of seeing God "face to face", and why we can speak of the eyes as "the windows of the soul". The body gives us access to the whole material world, and the most important and obvious and "alive" thing in our world is the sun, which we can feel with our whole bodies.

Second, the sun gives us light. Without light, we can see nothing, and physical seeing is our primary analogy or image for spiritual seeing or understanding.

Thus light is a universal symbol for truth. Truth is not merely correctness, the correspondence between an idea and a thing or a fact (though it is that, too). Truth is something real, something living, something alive, something that comes to us, like sunlight. In Heaven we will eat and drink truth; we will surf on it and swim in it. It will be more like liquid gold than like an equation.

Our human reason is the atmosphere God gave us to filter his infinite light. That is why mystical experience "works": it moves the filter away just a little bit, like raising the curtain between Heaven and earth an inch or so. As God invented our physical atmosphere in order that our bodies can receive sunlight in a safe, indirect, filtered way, so God also invented human reason, the human mind, so that we can receive truth in a filtered way. Human reason is the atmosphere for God's truth. Mystics are spiritual astronauts who take short trips beyond the atmosphere.

Science has discovered that in mystical experience the brain is not more active but less active. The part of the brain that does rational thinking, analysis, making distinctions, and calculations, the part we need and use to survive in a finite world, shuts down. It is as if the lid comes off a pot, releasing the smell of its food, or as if the dam is opened and more of the water of an infinite lake is released into the soul. In ordinary experience, the brain functions as a reducing valve, like the handle of a faucet or a garden hose, allowing us to cope with the small amounts of truth that we are capable of coping with rather than being flooded and drowned in the ocean of truth. It lets us calculate and distinguish and use the finite things of this world, including our own finite ego-selves. Mystical experience opens the valve for a short time, opens the faucet handle.

A very practical caution: there are two very different kinds of mysticism or mystical experiences: those that *we* do and those that God does, that God gives us. The first kind are dangerous and deceptive; the second kind are precious and good divine gifts. The greater any good thing is, the more dangerous and powerful its perversions or imitations are. Do-it-yourself mysticism, spiritual technologism, is like playing with fire or with bombs. Please never even think about venturing anywhere near a séance or a Ouija board! Even yoga can be suspect when it is not merely physical exercise. The Church warns us against fake and dangerous mysticisms like Reiki and "A Course in Miracles".

The following paragraph is a "stretch", and if you find it dangerous or heterodox, or simply unintelligible, just skip it and forgive me.

Time itself may be one of those reducing valves, since for God (and therefore in ultimate objective fact and truth and reality) nothing is dead past or unborn future but all is living present; and in mystical experience, we come closer to that "present-only" consciousness and see that time is part of the "reducing valve" by which we are enabled to separate and distinguish and deal with finite things. To God, everything is present at once and without confusion; and at the moment of death, we often get a glimpse of that, a vision of our whole life passing before us in a single instant that takes no time at all, that is not extended in time. And yet the things in our lives, in our past, that we see and feel in that sudden vision are not blurred or confused but seem brighter and clearer and more distinct than before, as well as more unified—a little bit more like the Persons of the Trinity.

(For a short and beautiful example of this mystical vision, read the most remarkable chapter [the shortest one] in a most remarkable novel, *Winter's Tale*, by Mark Helprin. If you saw the movie, try to forget it; the book is infinitely better.)

The third thing the sun gives us is warmth when we are cold. And the bodily warmth is a natural and God-intended symbol of spiritual warmth, which is love. Feel the warmth of the sun, which is one with and not an addition to its light and its life, as the Spirit and the Son, the *Logos*, are one with each other and with the Father.

In fact, God's love is infinitely more volcanic than the sun, and his "heat" would be unendurable

THE PRACTICAL "PAYOFF" 117

to us in our present fallen condition, so we need many filters to survive it and enjoy it. Time, space, and matter are those filters. They are the atmosphere that filters the rays of God's Sonlight. (All our knowledge of God is through his Son: cf. Jn 1:18.) Matter, time, and space both separate us from God, who transcends them, and also connect us to him, for he is also omnipresent in them. They are like hyphens, or breezeways, which both connect and separate, as our atmosphere both connects us to the sun and separates us from it.

The analogy of the atmosphere can be extended to everything in our lives. Divine Providence is the atmosphere for God's love to enter our lives. It spreads out God's single, eternal, and infinite love into our finite and plural time. It is like a prism that translates God's single, infinite, white light into finite and distinct colors.

That is the origin of beauty. Beauty is, to us, essentially a relationship between contrasting finite things. Colors are beautiful; light itself, which transcends color, is not in itself beautiful to us, but it is the source of all beauty, all colors. Light is to color what supernatural grace is to nature: not its rival, but its foundation and fulfillment. The more light, the more color.

When you pray in the sunlight, just be there and consciously and deliberately feel these gifts from God's sun, gifts that are being actively given to you now, at this sacred moment, from God himself. The sun is no accident; it is the icon of himself that God invented *for you*. Do you think he thinks more of gases and galaxies than he does of you? They are all there *for you*. This entire enormous universe was designed and created as your large playpen. Heaven is the larger house that surrounds it and contains it. You learn skills in the playpen that will mature and be used in the house, just as you learned skills in the womb that prepare you for life outside the womb. For instance, moving your hands and feet—what use do they have in the womb?

God is the fullness of life, and as the nature of the sun is to give you its rays, the nature of God is to give you life, in fact, not only natural life (*bios*) but a share in his supernatural life (*zoe*).

He is also light, or truth, and wants to give you truth, in fact, a share in his truth, his mind, first of all by divine revelation in this life, in his Church and in her Scriptures and dogmas and secondly in the next life by means whereof we have only the faintest hints, in the Beatific Vision, in which you shall see God's face and yet live.

The sun sends its light throughout the entire enormous universe. There is not a single area of space where its light absolutely stops. And this is true of every one of the trillions of stars. A telescope powerful enough could see the rays of light that came from the farthest star billions of years ago and that are only now arriving here. All the light of all the stars that shone in the past is present and visible everywhere in the universe in the present, at once. That is almost like God; it is a temporal and spatial and material image of God's ubiquitous omnipresence. And those stars just keep shining and shining and giving of themselves, almost forever—for billions of years, at least. That's only an "almost", and it is only finite, but it is a very big finite image of the infinitely bigger God, the God who is the source of all life, light, and love.

He is love, too, and is even now giving you rays of his love, caressing your spirit, smiling at you, affirming you, praising you as his child, loving you not only dearly but eternally and infinitely and beyond all price. (Look at the price he paid to save you!)

Like the Persons of the Trinity, life, light, and love are three and yet one. They are one in two ways. They are one in the single essential *nature* of God. And they are also one as the three divine Persons are one in the personal relationship of the mutual self-giving by each of the Persons to the others.

This high and palmy theology is extremely practical because this God is our whole future hope and happiness; this is the God whose life we will actually share and be caught up into in Heaven, if our deepest will, our "fundamental option", is to will his will. And that is why "in his will is our peace." T. S. Eliot calls that line from Dante the most profound line in literature.

※

There is another practical payoff of the truth of the Trinity that is connected to the Eucharist.

What happens when we receive the Eucharist? What do we get?

We get God! We get The Supreme, Infinite, Eternal, Incomprehensible Being/Truth/Love. We get the substance, the objective reality, of our heavenly joy, though we are as far from understanding it, appreciating it, feeling it, or rightly responding to it as a dollhouse teaspoon is far from containing all the water of the sea.

And since God is the Trinity of infinite being, knowing, and goodwilling; of life, light, and love; therefore *that* is what we get when we receive him in the Eucharist. We literally need absolutely nothing else.

The Father and the Spirit did not become incarnate, but the Son did, and all of the Godhead is present and available to us in him. All of it. Jesus "is it". Jesus is the whole revelation of God, "that's all there is, there ain't no more!" (That's what Colossians 1:19 explicitly says.) He gives us his Father and his Spirit, too, when he gives us himself.

THE PRACTICAL "PAYOFF" 121

Pope Benedict was asked by a rabbi the challenging question: What difference did Jesus make? The world before his coming was sinful, sorrowful, selfish, stupid, and suffering, diseased, and dying, full of faithlessness and hopelessness and lovelessness, of oppression and war and hate and murder. And now, 2000 years later, the world is still full of every single one of those awful things. So what difference did Jesus make? What did he give us that we didn't have before?

And like a child, the pope answered in one syllable. God. He gave us God.

And that is what we get in Holy Communion. We get the total life-light-love that is the essence of God. The meaning of all things is placed on our tongue. We eat the meaning of life.

Another eminently practical difference the Trinity makes to our lives is that it is the definitive answer to the problem of suffering, the problem of pain.

That problem is both theoretical and practical.

It is theoretical because it is the strongest argument for atheism. If God exists, why do we suffer? Why are we not happy? If God (1) really exists and (2) loves us and therefore wants us to be happy and (3) knows what will make us happy and (4) has the power to do anything, then why are we not happy? Must not God be either nonexistent, unloving, ignorant, or impotent?

The problem is also practical because pain (both physical and emotional) is intensely practical. When we are in pain, the thing we want the most is not a theoretical explanation, however perfect, but relief. Sermons cannot take the place of drugs any more than drugs can take the place of sermons.

And God the Trinity answers both the theoretical and practical problem of suffering. The theoretical answer is the infallible argument that the four divine attributes mentioned in the atheist's argument above are all real and unlimited, and therefore it necessarily and logically follows that the most wonderful and hard-to-believe verse in the whole Bible (Rom 8:28) must be true: that all things, without exception, even the things that are the farthest from being good, must work together for the greater good for all who love and trust God. He conquers all obstacles; he saves us from everything and does not allow any evil to come into our lives unless he sees that it will work out for an even greater good in the end than if it did not exist.

That's why he allowed the most horrible thing that ever happened, the torture and murder of his own Son. That is our paradigmatic and definitive answer to the problem of evil. As Aquinas says, quoting Augustine, "[God] would not allow any evil to exist in his works unless his omnipotence and

THE PRACTICAL "PAYOFF"

goodness were such as to bring good even out of evil." That is the only possible answer to the strongest argument for atheism.

Because we have free will, free choice, we can refuse to believe and hope and love and trust God and receive this incredible gift. So *not* all things work together for good in the end to *everyone*, automatically. Only for those who love God. God loves everyone, but not everyone loves him and what he is (Truth and Love). "The end" for some is Hell, not Heaven. Yes, there is a Hell as well as a Heaven, if Jesus is not a fool or a liar. But we have no idea of their comparative population statistics, and Christ himself refused to answer that question: see Luke 13:23–24.

Just look at the work of the Trinity to see the necessary truth of Romans 8:28.

God the Father is infinite, unlimited power. He created the entire universe, and all the angels, from absolutely nothing, with no help or need or even effort. He confronts no obstacles.

God the Son is infinite, unlimited wisdom, the Mind of God, the *Logos*, the Total Truth. He cannot make a mistake. He is the Father's total and infallible knowledge of himself. He *understands* everything totally and completely, including the unendurable agony we sometimes suffer in body, soul, and spirit, and what agonies and sorrows will work out for our greater good and joy.

God the Holy Spirit is infinite, unlimited love of, for, and between Father and Son. He cannot not-love. He cannot hate or even be indifferent. God is not a Stoic. God weeps with us. (Jn 11:35: this is God's first and immediate answer to the problem of our pain.) He is with us always (Mt 28:20), because that is what love does. Love never forsakes, even when it seems to (Mt 27:46).

We can doubt any one of these three truths. We can reduce the Father to an engineer, God the Son to a philosophy professor, and God the Holy Spirit to a pop psychologist, if we choose to be utter fools and try to edit or correct God's own revelation to us. We can try to change places with God, but it won't work, because even though we can very easily reduce God to our own size in our own minds, we cannot enlarge our size to his.

What makes all these incredible practical consequences possible is that the three Persons are one God, that they actively cooperate (literally "work together"). It is only because the Father, the Son, and the Holy Spirit work together in all things for our greatest good that "all things work together for good" for us if we love him. For in him, Being (Power, Life), Knowing (*Logos*, Light, Truth), and Love *are one thing*, not three things. His love is his whole being, and his whole being is love. His knowledge is his whole being, and his whole being is knowledge.

It is a remarkable empirical fact that everyone who has ever had a deep near-death experience or out-of-body experience and met the "Being of Light" that greeted them on the other side has implicitly confirmed this Trinitarian theology, though not in explicit words, because they all said the same thing about this experience, even though their religious beliefs differed and the interpretations and explanations they used for this "Being of Light" differed. They all said that from this Being came the same two things: total knowledge and total love; that he knew them totally and absolutely and loved them totally and absolutely. Though they did not usually put it into such abstract philosophical terms, they said that his being, his knowing, and his loving were one, because the knowing was one with the loving and that both were inseparable from his being. Technically and philosophically put, knowledge and love are not accidents or acts added to God's being. They are his being; they are what he *is*, not just what he *does*. He could stop doing what he does, but he cannot stop being what he is.

(By instructive contrast, that is the thing Sartre's atheism explicitly denies, especially in his most famous work, the play *No Exit*: that it is possible to love a person even when you know his faults. For

Sartre, our two distinctively human powers, knowing and loving, contradict each other. They move in opposite directions. And therefore the idea of a God who both knows and loves us is impossible. That was also Nietzsche's deepest reason for atheism: that he could not endure a God who knew all of him, even his "dark side". Love, to Nietzsche, is pity, and weakness. Love was the great danger.)

The people who experienced this "Being of Light" also all changed their philosophy of life (though not always their religion) after this experience, and in a remarkably similar way. (Cf. *Life after Life* by Raymond A. Moody, Jr., M.D.) They now all knew that there are only two absolute values, only two things that count eternally and totally: truth and love, understanding and loving. Everything else is negotiable and mortal; these two things are nonnegotiable and immortal. They are the whole meaning of life.

This wisdom, this realization, this wonderful simplification of values, that transformed the minds and philosophies of all those who met the Being of Light did not make them automatic or instant saints. But it did make them simple and wise.

And they lost all fear of death. They knew they were "absolutely safe", as Wittgenstein put it. Because the Being that is in charge of life and death, the Being that is stronger than death, the Absolute Being, knows them completely and absolutely and loves them completely and absolutely.

And there is simply nothing imaginable or desirable that is better than that. That is the Goodest Good News conceivable. Our wildest fantasies and our dreamiest dreams cannot hold a candle to that light. Truth and goodness are one, so it is no longer possible to believe that it is "too good to be true". That is the practical payoff of Trinitarian Christian theology.

APPENDIX I
A Revolutionary Metaphysics

This is an appendix for philosophers. But we are all philosophers. If you say you have no philosophy, that is your philosophy: a bad one.

The philosophical consequences of the Trinitarian union of being, truth, and love that we have explored seem to me immense, especially in the primary and most fundamental division of philosophy, namely, metaphysics, which is about being.

Metaphysics is not about what is beyond ("meta") physics in the sense that it is only about that which is non-physical or spiritual, or about that which is supernatural rather than natural. It is about everything. It is "beyond" in scope, size, extension, or universality. It is about what the word "being" means.

What is the meaning of being? Is it essence, existence, oneness, substance, form, actuality, potentiality, mystery, or what? (See Gilson's magisterial *Being and Some Philosophers* for a very profound survey of some of the answers to that ultimate question that the history of philosophy has offered us.) And the ultimate answer, the "bottom line", of metaphysics, if the dogma of the Trinity is true, seems to be ...

Wait for it. The world waited thousands of years for it. And now we have it. We have it in the life and ministry and teachings of Jesus, and we have it in the teachings of his Church and of her New Testament, and we have it in the Eucharist, and we have it in the lives of the saints. Here it is: *To be is to love*. Being is loving. Love is not just a human feeling or even just a human choice or even just an absolute value or commandment. *Love is the nature of being*. The more loving a being is, the more real it is.

Everything that has some kind of being has some kind of loving. The Thomist philosopher Jacques Maritain speaks of "ontological (metaphysical) generosity". What he means by that is that everything that exists *gives* itself to some other beings. The very being of the mountain stands between and separates what is on its north and south sides. It is acting (though not moving through space) both to join and to separate north and south. It gives some new being to something else, it makes a real difference to something else, and therefore it is participating in some kind of cosmic generosity, some sort of cosmic love, "the love that moves the sun and the other stars".

Gravity is love on the level of matter. Love is gravity on the level of spirit.

And the aim of all love is unity, with-ness, in-ness. (See Appendix 2.)

This notion, of every being giving itself, yielding itself, sacrificing itself to another, is strikingly similar to the metaphysics of Taoism in the *Tao Te Ching*, which Orthodox Hieromonk Damascene, in *Christ the Eternal Tao*, called the closest approximation in all of paganism to the Christian understanding of the essential nature of God.

Everything gives and receives something, some love. That is how everything lives and moves and has its being. That is also how we live and move and have our being. And it is how we succeed in our fundamental task, how we flourish, how we attain joy and peace and glory. To give love and receive love are the two things that make us most subjectively happy and objectively perfect and complete.

Thus the whole Christian ethic of love is grounded in the nature of ultimate reality as the Trinity. Because God is a Trinity, God is love, and because God is love, love "goes all the way up" into ultimate reality. The practical point is grounded in the theoretical point. Love is our *ethical* absolute because it is the *metaphysical* absolute. It is good because it is true. Nothing is "too good to be true".

Thus we are to "be holy *because* I the LORD am holy." We must be good because Being himself is good, because goodness is not just ethical but metaphysical, because it is real. Being good is being true to reality.

Plato dimly perceived this unity of metaphysics and ethics when he labelled the ultimate reality, not Being or Oneness or Essence or Truth, but The Good.

But Plato did not know that it was interpersonal love. He thought it was an abstract essence, the *object* of love (the good, the lovable), but not love itself. It was infinite and eternal and absolute, but it was not a Person or a God.

Socrates came closer. He said (in the *Symposium*) that love was the only thing he claimed to know about. He also believed in and obeyed and became a martyr for his monotheism, for his one God, the "unknown God" (*agnosto theo*), which is probably the exact description Saint Paul discovered on an altar without a statue when he preached to the Greek philosophers on Mars Hill in Athens (Acts 17:16–34). Socrates was a stonecutter and may have actually cut that inscription. And Saint Paul gave the humble and God-seeking disciples of Socrates an immense encouragement when he said that "what therefore you worship as unknown, this I proclaim to you" (v. 23). The verb he used for "worship", *eusebeite*, is not in the aorist tense, which designates a single action, but in the present progressive tense, which designates ongoing and habitual action.

Socrates not only believed in and worshipped (although in ignorance) the true God but also died for him as well as living for him (he never questioned or disobeyed the *daimon* or spirit that he called his "divine voice"). He was executed only because he could not honestly say that he believed in any of the gods of the State and was therefore declared an atheist, a heretic, a corrupter of the youth, and a noncitizen by the jury that convicted and condemned him.

That statement of Saint Paul affirming and approving the Athenians' God-seeking is an implicit equation between the God Socrates sought and the God Saint Paul found. Interpreted in light of Saint John's equation of Christ with the *Logos*, or ultimate truth sought by the philosophers, it is the foundation of the fundamental intellectual enterprise of Christendom, the civilization that was to emerge and produce the Middle Ages. That enterprise was the marriage between Athens and Jerusalem, reason and faith, Socrates and Jesus, the marriage that is now in deep divorce and the advanced stages of cultural suicide.

That culture, Christendom, came into being primarily through love, sanctity, and martyrdom, not through philosophy. It can resurrect, even after it dies, because it is immortal. It is the culture not of a State but a Church, and it is immortal because that Church is the Body of Christ, the resurrected

Christ. But in order for it to resurrect, it will have to love so much and so well that it is willing to die and be martyred again. If it does, nothing can defeat it because nothing can defeat divine love, the love that is stronger than death and is the essential nature of Ultimate Reality.

Meanwhile, a philosophy that acknowledges the metaphysical basis for this cultural revolution by identifying Being (God) with Loving (*Agape*), though merely a philosophy and thus not sufficient by itself, is an extremely helpful and probably necessary intellectual foundation for a culture of life and light and love to replace our present culture of death and darkness and despair. The divorce of love from Being, of ethics from metaphysics, of the good from the true—the moral relativism and nihilism of our present culture—has torn us from God, that is, from our ultimate root and First Cause and our ultimate end and hope. Only repentance and remarriage will bring us back. Only saints can save the world. The reason that is true is in the Trinitarian theology of Christianity.

APPENDIX II

On "IN"

I think it was Kierkegaard who remarked that if we only understood all the meanings of the word "in" there would be no mysteries left in Christian theology.

God is "in" the world, and the world is also "in" God. The Father is "in" the Son, and the Son is "in" the Father. We are "in" the Spirit, and the Spirit is "in" us. Christ is "in" his Church, and the Church is "in" Christ. We are "in" the Church, and the Church is "in" us.

The only two things that are not in fact "in" each other are good and evil. There is no evil in true goodness, and there is no goodness in evil.

There is indeed "a little good in the worst of us and a little bad in the best of us so that it ill behooves the best of us to speak ill of the worst of us", as Thornton Wilder wrote, but there is no goodness in evil and no evil in goodness. But everything else is in some way "in" everything else.

The Chinese (Taoist, Confucian, and Buddhist) philosophy of yin and yang being universally "in" each other is correct about other things, but not about moral good and evil. It is true of life and death, pleasure and pain, worldly failure and success, good luck and bad luck, but not of virtue and vice. God does not have a dark side. "God is light and in him is no darkness at all" (1 Jn 1:5).

So there is a nearly universal "in-ness". But while on the literal and material level, A cannot be "in" B and also B "in" A at the same time (either a city is enclosed by a country or a country is enclosed by a city), yet on the spiritual level A can be "in" B in one way while B is also "in" A in another way, as in all the examples in our second paragraph above. Our sensory imagination is helpful in providing analogies for spiritual things, but it habitually deceives us and tempts us to error when we take it literally rather than symbolically and analogically—which nearly everyone now is coming to do, now that computers have almost abolished our comprehension of analogies. Analogies are the one kind of thinking computers are totally incapable of, and analogies are also probably the single most basic and primordial foundation of human intelligence. God designed our senses and our sensory imagination to be a useful image, icon, or analogy for spiritual things.

So let us begin with the literal, physical, spatial meaning of "in" as an analogy of spiritual "in-ness".

One thing is "in" another when it is surrounded by it. Think of two circles, A and B, one enclosing the other. There are two possible situations: A is "in" B or B is "in" A. Both are possible at once only if "in" is not univocal (one meaning only) but analogical (two or more related meanings)—which is not possible in Euclidean geometry.

There are also three and only three other logically possible relationships between A and B. A and B could be identical, like twelves and dozens, or they could be totally separate, like light and darkness, or they could be partially overlapping, like the two classes of truths, truths known by faith and truths known by reason.

When we think of the relationship between God the Creator and his creatures, between spirit and matter, between body and soul, between Christ and his Church, between the sacred and the secular, or between God's consciousness and mine, we must think, whether explicitly or implicitly, in terms of one of these five possible relationships, and usually it comes down to the first two: either A is "in" B or B is "in" A.

But we habitually think inside out. We think of God as an entity that, together with other entities, stands "in" the whole of being; that is, we think of God as "a" being rather than as Being itself. We think of ourselves and our Creator as two of the characters "in" a greater whole. But the truth is the opposite: God is not "in" our world (except by the Incarnation), or part of our world, or "in" our religious experience; we are "in him" and parts of his world and in his "religious experience".

And we think of the sacred as a part of our secular, worldly experience. Cathedrals are "in" secular nations; their sacred space and times are enclosed by secular spaces and times. But this too is inside out. Everything, including the secular, is sacred, but not everything is secular. The sacred is not secular, but the secular is sacred.

We think of the sacred, the holy, the religious, the transcendent, or the supernatural as one of the dimensions of the secular, or the natural. But this is backwards, because everything is sacred, while not everything is secular. Our secular "stuff" is part of our sacred "stuff". Cathedrals are "in" the secular world physically, but they are built to remind us that the whole cosmos is a cathedral. Sacred times are set aside to remind us that all times are sacred. We are enclosed by the sacred; we do not enclose it, except as an iconic reminder to the fallen consciousness. In Heaven, human consciousness is no longer fallen; that is why there is no need for temples there: see Revelation 21:22.

Because we are "in" and "surrounded by" God, everything, without exception, is "in" God's providential plan, including all evil things, which, though they originated "outside" God's will, by the misuse of angelic and human free wills, are nevertheless divinely and infallibly foreseen and wisely allowed and integrated into and used by the divine plan for the greatest good, which "encloses" and uses even these evils. Thus "in everything [even evil things] God works for [the greater] good with those who love him [trust him, believe him, accept his will and his providential plan], who are called according to his [overall, all-inclusive teleological] purpose" (Rom 8:28).

This is the single simple solution to the problem of evil. Good is not surrounded by evil; evil is surrounded by good. Good is not relative to evil; evil is relative to good. Good is not defined by evil; evil is defined by good. All is "in" God's plan. Thus Aquinas solves the problem of evil by saying that "[God] would not allow any evil to exist in his works unless his omnipotence and goodness were such as to bring good even out of evil." The paradigm case of this, of course, is "Good" Friday, the most evil thing that ever happened, the deliberate, hateful torture and murder of Almighty God, the "death of God". And that greatest of evils gave us the greatest of goods, salvation from eternal misery and the hope of infinite joy.

Here is another surprise about in-ness. It's about the relation between matter and spirit and, within us, soul and body. We think of the soul as "in"

the body, but Aquinas corrects us and says the body is "in" the soul. Descartes foolishly tried to locate the soul "in" the body and "in" the brain, and "in" the pineal gland. To see why this is mistaken, consider the analogue of a play. (Life is like a play, or, rather, a play is like life.) In a play, its body, its physical setting, its stage sets are only one dimension of or "in" the play. The other dimensions are either spiritual (its meaning, its values, the teleology of its plot) or both spiritual and physical (its characters and their actions). We think inside out if we think that a play takes place "in" its setting. That is true physically, of course, but the setting itself, and all the physical actions in it, are themselves "in" the play, which is a work of art, that is, a work of the human spirit.

Within a human individual, there is clearly a real distinction between the body and the soul. The body is material and takes up space and can be measured by material and quantitative categories such as size and speed and kinetic energy. The soul does not take up space and cannot be measured by such quantities. The soul is capable of intentional thinking, that is, reason (understanding, judging, and proving), while the body is not. Computers, which have no soul, do not think; they are only mobile books that record and imitate and encode and communicate the results of human thinking. But we habitually think of the soul as "in" the body, either in part of the body (the brain) or, better, diffused throughout the body. But the body is in the soul rather than the soul in the body. The analogy of the play, above, explains why, and we can intuit that immediately, in a flash, in a glance, if the power of analogical thinking has not yet quite fully expired in us.

When we think about God, love God, believe God, and sometimes feel God, we think that God is "in" our consciousness or our experience. (By the way, how remarkable it is that when we say "experience", we almost always mean "feel" rather than "think" or "will".) But God is far too "large" to fit there. Rather, we are in him, we are "in" his consciousness and love and, perhaps, his spiritual "feelings", if that category is in some way accurate. We usually think of God as "in" or part of our life, but we are "in" or parts of God's life. The finite is "in" the infinite rather than the infinite Being "in" the finite. (The infinite, however, can be the *object* of the finite when the finite is "intentional," i.e., when it thinks *about* something true or loves something good.)

So what does all this have to do with the Trinity?

If God is only one Person, there is no plurality in him. Thus plurality, for the Unitarian, is like matter: it is in the creation but not in the Creator, who is only one and not many in any way. So plurality is less than oneness, less divine, less valuable, less real than oneness.

But plurality is in fact real and valuable because God created it. And "you can't give what you don't have", so if plurality is of any value, it must be in God also. And it *is* of value, great value. It makes possible individuality and otherness and relationship and fellowship—and love!

If God is only one, and there is no plurality in him, then love, which presupposes plurality, is not a value that goes all the way up into God. It is not the supreme value. To reach God, we must transcend it. It can be a value only in creatures but not in the Creator. What kind of a loveless God is that?

If God has no plurality in his being, then God is oneness only. So then to be one and alone is of more value than to be loved and lover. What kind of God is that? What kind of religion is that? It is what Plotinus called "the flight of the alone to the Alone". That sounds more like Hell than like Heaven.

This is Neo-Platonism, which, in the form of Gnosticism, is the heresy that most bedeviled Christian thinkers throughout history and is doing so again today. "I'm spiritual but not religious" is modern man's credo. For "religion" means, literally, "binding relationship". Marriage is its greatest and most important instance. And we all know what is happening to marriage throughout our culture.

Because God is a Trinity, plurality, relationship, love, and personality, go all the way up and have supreme, infinite, eternal, and absolute value. And so do "in-ness" and "with-ness". They too are transcendentals, or universals, like goodness, truth, and beauty. To be is to be with; *esse est co-esse*—in us creatures because it is in the Creator.

APPENDIX III

A Trinitarian Feminism

Another revolutionary corollary of this Trinitarianism is that *receiving* being, love, and value is also of absolute value. The Father receives love from the Son as well as giving it, and the Son receives love from the Father as well as giving it. Thus just as personality and plurality and love are aspects of the perfect divine nature, receptivity is, too, as well as activity.

It is a biological fact that in reproduction the female anatomy is teleologically ordered to receiving and the male anatomy to giving. And it is a psychological fact that the soul and the body are psychosomatically one substance, not two. We are not ghosts in machines or animals and angels tied together. The conclusion from these two premises is that femininity and masculinity are spiritual as well as physical.

The body reflects and images the soul. It is not an alien other, a part of the impersonal world. It is part of our personality. Our "personality" in the sense of our personhood (and our "personality" in the popular sense, also, our emotional toolkit) is in our bodies as well as our souls. And just as our bodies all have both male and female hormones, our souls have both feminine (receptive) and masculine (active) powers. Creativity always requires the union of both.

Therefore the feminine, the womblike, the receptive, on both the physical and the spiritual level, is of equal value with the masculine, the phallic, the initiative. And this is grounded in the fact that receptivity as well as activity are in the Trinity.[1]

Thus, Trinitarianism is the ultimate and most radical feminism.

---

[1] A woman need not deny her distinctive feminine *nature* in order to affirm her equal *value* vis-à-vis men. Equality in value does not require equality in nature. Every culture in history has noticed that women's souls, like their bodies, specialize in the receptive virtues. Unfortunately, most cultures have also believed that receptivity is inferior to activity, because they have confused "first act" (actual existence) with "second act" (operation, work). Actual being is indeed superior to potential being, but pitchers are not superior to catchers, nor are men superior to women. But they are (gloriously) *different*.